CONQUERING
THE
SAT

*How Parents Can
Help Teens Overcome
the Pressure and Succeed*

NED JOHNSON & EMILY WARNER ESKELSEN

First published in 2007 by
PALGRAVE MACMILLAN™
175 Fifth Avenue, New York, N.Y. 10010 and
Houndmills, Basingstoke, Hampshire, England RG21 6XS.
Companies and representatives throughout the world.

PALGRAVE MACMILLAN is the global academic imprint of the
Palgrave Macmillan division of St. Martin's Press, LLC and of Palgrave
Macmillan Ltd. Macmillan® is a registered trademark in the United
States, United Kingdom and other countries. Palgrave is a registered
trademark in the European Union and other countries.

ISBN-13: 978-1-4039-7667-3
ISBN-10: 1-4039-7667-8

Library of Congress Cataloging-in-Publication Data

Johnson, Ned.
   Conquering the SAT : how parents can help teens overcome the
pressure and succeed / Ned Johnson and Emily Warner Eskelson.
      p.   cm.
   Includes bibliographical references and index.
   ISBN 1-4039-7667-8 (alk. paper)
   1. SAT (Educational test)   2. Education—Parent participation—
United States.   I. Eskelson, Emily Warner.   II. Title.

LB2353.57.J645   2007
378.1'662—dc22

                                                            2006049490

A catalogue record of the book is available from the British Library.

Design by Letra Libre, Inc.

First edition: January, 2007
10 9 8 7 6 5 4 3 2 1
Printed in the United States of America.

"*Conquering the SAT* offers insightful commentary about the nature of standardized testing and the value that we place upon it in American society. More importantly, though, it illuminates unique strategies for parents who want to learn the ins and outs of the college admissions hierarchy and get their kids to the top of it . . ."

—*Paul Moskowitz, former PrepMatters student*

"I went to Ned in the middle of my junior year in high school. I had never been a great test taker, but set high goals for myself on the SAT. During my first tutoring session, Ned told me to take the pressure off of myself by placing the SAT in its proper context . . . I can honestly say that I would not have made it through the SAT without him."

—*Austin Clarke, Yale University*

"As a PrepMatters alumna, I can proudly say that Johnson and Warner's methods helped to improve my score by nearly 300 points. With their guidance I learned how to overcome my test anxiety, and gained both important skills and the confidence I needed to truly conquer the SATs. The college process was significantly less stressful for both me and my family thanks to their instruction."

—*Anna Salzberg, Kenyon College*

"Ned Johnson approaches SAT preparation from a uniquely individual perspective. By breaking down each section of the test into a step by step process, Ned has demystified this test. His strategies help students find a clear and specific approach and give them confidence to do their best on this most stressful test. High school students should begin their studying with this book."

—*Rhona M. Gordon, M.S., C.C.C.,*
ASHA Certified Speech/Language Pathologist

"Ned taught me skills and strategies that I will use forever and most importantly built my confidence which dramatically enhanced my performance on tests."

—*Mia Ferrara, Georgetown University*

"Although Ned Johnson certainly taught both of my children valuable strategies for facing down the PSATs and the SATs, he distinguished himself in this mother's heart by caring for them as individuals and giving them concrete ways to combat anxiety so it did not interfere with their performances on these dreaded tests. Ned was a cheerleader and friend to my children at a time when they sorely needed an objective adult in their lives telling them that they *could* succeed at this! He also helped us—parents and children alike—keep the *meaning of the test* in a very healthy perspective."

—*Linda Reider, mother of Suzanne and Rob, Bowdoin College*

"Through tremendous personal dedication to the mastery of the SAT, Ned has put himself into the minds of the student and the ETS to provide exclusive tactics on how to excel on America's most important test . . . Like a marathon trainer, Ned coaches students mentally and physically for the long race ahead. His qualifications are top-notch, his advice fresh, and his results unsurpassed."

—*Melissa Giamo, Pepperdine University*

"An indispensable survival guide for all parents of SAT test-takers."

—*Julia Novitch, Yale University*

As every human interaction offers the opportunity to teach or to learn, I thank my students from whom I have learned so much and to whom I hope I have provided some wisdom that lingers beyond the days of standardized tests and vocabulary cards.

Vanessa, thank you for rowing with me and for long ago steering me to a passion that so fulfills me. Matthew and Katie, I wish you every success, but above all nurture your character and passionately pursue your dreams. I love you.

Ned

To my absentee soldier husband and my ever-present little children.

E.W.E.

Contents

Note from the Authors

It has been a privilege and a pleasure for both of us to work with such lovely young people and their families over the years. We are grateful for their many and indispensable contributions to the production of this book and sincerely hope that our offering will be of service to the next generation of college-bound students and their families.

Within these pages, we employ many examples of families with whom we have interacted. With great respect, we share their experiences for the benefit of all. Naturally, names and details of the personal stories contained herein have been altered to protect identities. Further, as the stories we share are far from extraordinary, we have taken the liberty of creating fictionalized composite students who best exemplify traits and experiences we've seen again and again over the past decade. Parents and students may recognize characteristics they share or parts of experiences they've had, and we hope that does in fact happen as families use this book to develop healthier and more successful testing habits. While we have tutored children from prominent and recognizable families, none of the stories in this book are literally drawn from one family or one student and should not be read as such.

Finally, we would like to be clear that we come at the subject of the SAT from the perspective of tutors. We are experts in the test and in student reactions to the test. We are not clinical diagnosticians; nor are we medical or psychological professionals in any sense. One on one with a student, we can usually provide specific insights and advice for that student's testing needs. Over the years, we've noticed trends and patterns, and would like to share what we've learned, as educational professionals. Nothing in this book should be taken as medical, psychiatric, or legal advice. Instead, please use our insights to help guide you in your quest for a healthier, happier, and more successful teen.

I

Introduction

It was the morning of the SAT. The clock ticked 8:20 AM, and the room began to get restless. The girls in front of me giggled too loudly while someone behind me began a nervous foot-tapping routine. The guy to my left fiddled with his calculator abruptly. I listened in on the test-oriented conversation behind me—"Should I skip a question if I'm not sure?" I thought of turning around to add my two cents and then thought better of it. The air in the classroom was stale with chalk and ammonia. The proctor walked into the room, and conversation stilled expectantly. She was fiftyish, a central casting's view of an English teacher, graying and solid. The students peered at her apprehensively, knowing a whim on her part could cheat them of minutes on their exam or deprive them of a precious five-minute break. Shuffling some papers, she glanced at the clock and then walked back out. The clock ticked 8:35 AM, well past the 8:15 deadline for all test-takers to report to their classrooms. "Why is this taking so long?" I heard muttered around me, "What's going on?"

The conversations around me grew tighter, more strained. The anxiety became more palpable. I smiled to myself. Poor kids, I thought, this is a big test for them. Free associating, I wondered what was going through their minds, how their anxiety was taking its course. Shallow breathing? Panic? Racing heartbeats? For no particular reason, I checked my own pulse. 140 beats per minute—what the heck? I hadn't felt nervous. Or had I?

Anxiety—It's the wild card of all performance. You know you know the material. You know you can make the shot. You've hit that high note over and over again in countless rehearsals. Somehow, when it comes time to put your pencil to the paper, your mind goes blank. You miss the shot. You choke on the note. Your mind reels with a flood of thoughts, your face goes hot, and somehow it feels like everyone in the room is staring at you. You panic! Every doubt you've ever had comes rushing in, accompanied by every perceived insult to your intelligence or ability. You feel like a failure. Why is this happening?

As a professional tutor for the SAT, I've taken the SAT many times and logged over 25,000 hours preparing others to take the SAT and various standardized tests. I coach others on what to expect and how to excel. So after all my years of test-taking and test-teaching, it always seems inexplicable to me that I should be nervous. If even an expert on tests and test-taking can be nervous, imagine what it's like for a 16-year-old his first time "at bat."

The SAT claims a disproportionate amount of our collective anxiety. This test carries so much emotional baggage that just a mention of it can cause college graduates to shudder. Adults well past their educational years still remember and compare their scores. The SAT is the most recognizable test name in America; this is the test that matters most to Americans. This is the test that causes American teenagers the most anxiety.

If there's one thing high school students know, it's tests. They've been taking tests steadily for 12 years, and they know that you have to get almost everything right to get an A on a test. The SAT changes the rules of testing: a scaled SAT has two-thirds of all students receiving what would be, on a normal high school test, a failing grade. Worse, the test is timed so that even some above-average students don't finish. Factor in all sorts of conflicting advice about skipping questions and point penalties, and who can blame the poor kids for panicking?

In addition, the SAT is a fatiguing test, nearly four hours long. That's a lot of time for morning cereal to sustain a growing teenager. That's a lot of time to get discouraged, tired, or distracted. That's a lot of time for a test-taker to replay the constant tape recorder in his head:

"You're no good at tests—you always panic—your sister is smarter than you . . ." and so on. This tape recording, the baggage a test-taker carries with him, may be the most significant factor in determining the likelihood that anxiety will be a major factor in his test experience and test results.

When it comes down to it, anxiety is any factor, other than knowledge and skill, that affects test-taking. It's self-doubt. It's adrenaline. It's fed by peer and parental pressures, personal expectations, past experiences, future goals, and, in the case of teenagers, who is sitting next to you during the test and did your friends notice you didn't finish? It's all the factors that make up attitude and performance on the test. Part of anxiety is a student's innate reaction to a stressful situation, and part is an acculturated response to external pressures.

Strangely enough, anxiety is not in itself a bad thing. We need that rush of adrenaline to make that lay-up as the buzzer is sounding, and we need the pressure to study and be prepared when the results matter. That part of anxiety that feeds effort and performance is a necessary component to success. Later this book will explore ways parents and students can identify and channel that energy into productive test-taking.

The part of anxiety we *don't* need is the part that whispers self-doubt. We don't need sibling and peer comparisons, or overwhelming feelings of worthlessness. We don't need the paralysis of feeling incapable, or the mania of panic to compensate. These parts of anxiety aren't biological or natural—they are external, environmental, and conquerable. This book can help parents and, as a result, their teens discover the sources of this anxiety and learn how to eradicate it.

As the authors have done for so many students, we'd like to help make the SAT a positive, successful experience—one that not only helps students achieve their college entrance goals, but also helps them build up the experience and confidence they need to be successful, independent adults. That is, after all, why we wrote this book: to show parents how they can help teens find a better, healthier, more successful way to take the SAT.

The SAT

Standardized Testing and Underperformance

CHAPTER ONE

ETS *and the* SAT

What do you get if you combine six haystacks with seven haystacks?
How many three-cent stamps are in a dozen?
How much dirt is in a hole two feet wide, two feet long, and two feet deep?
A farmer had six sick sheep. All but two died. How many are left?
I have two coins totaling 30 cents. One is not a nickel. What are they?[1]

Heard these before? Chances are if you're good at these puzzlers, you'd have a leg up if you were to take the SAT. There's one big difference between the mind teasers above and SAT questions: on the questions above, you know someone's trying to fool you. On the SAT, most kids don't realize that the maker of the SAT, Educational Testing Service (ETS), is playing with their minds.

Let me illustrate with another puzzler. Try the following in your head as quickly as possible: start with 1000. Add 40. Add 1000. Add 30. Add 1000. Add 20. Add 1000. Add 10. What number did you get? Are you sure about that? Did you get 5000? So do most people, but most people are wrong. Using simple mathematics, this problem tricked you into a false deduction; essentially, you were led to select an incorrect answer on a problem well within your ability to solve correctly. Before adding the final ten, your total was 4090. Without a calculator or pencil and paper, it was too easy for your mind to use the final ten to round up to 5000, instead of the correct answer, 4100.

Math puzzles may be silly and pointless—just entertainment—but what if we had prefaced this question by telling you that your answer would greatly influence the course of your education and, by implication, your entire future?

And that you would be timed.

The situation is a little different now, isn't it? And, some may say, a bit unfair. After all, wouldn't it be more serviceable to test actual mathematical skill than to attempt to trap test-takers into making false assumptions? True, you won't see a problem like the one above on any SAT for several reasons, but you will see students making the same kind of false deduction on question after question on the test. In fact, the SAT is designed just so that will happen.

The popular (but generally false) perception is that the SAT is "hard" because it tests advanced concepts in verbal and mathematics skills. The SAT *is* a tough test, but not because the material it covers is difficult or particularly advanced. In fact, many high school students find the math sections challenging in part because the concepts are comparatively remedial to their current mathematics classes.

The SAT is a tough test precisely for the reasons that the above math problem tricks so many intelligent people: we're not expecting to be tested *in that way*. We are drawn into the problem because it seems manageable and straightforward, yet our confident answers turn out to be incorrect, time and again. To understand the psychology of the SAT, we must understand what happened when we added those numbers in our heads, and why that problem is so universally successful. To fathom what our children taking the SAT experience, we must first discover what lies at the crux of the most famous test in American education. We must learn what the SAT is all about.

WHO IS ETS?

You might think that the ETS offices in Princeton, New Jersey, are populated by retired math teachers, English professors, and educators of all sorts. One imagines heated staff meetings discussing the state of college preparatory curriculums in this country and the role of standardized testing in staving off intellectual illiteracy. And perhaps that does happen.

What you might not imagine, however, are the bristling crowds of educational psychologists, psychometricians, and statisticians—experts in making tests and predicting results—in those very offices, and the significant role these scientists play in constructing the test that more American teenagers take than any other. In reality, ETS is a quite profitable nonprofit organization made up of test-writing experts plotting out predictions and manipulations of teenage testing behavior.

This is neither shocking nor a secret. ETS is the best at what it does, and what it does is rank millions of high school juniors and seniors according to an agreed-upon standardized system: the SAT. Creating and administering a widespread and complicated ranking system simply isn't the province of high school geometry teachers or literature buffs. Never mind that the SAT has gone through numerous and somewhat drastic permutations throughout the years. Never mind that "SAT" no longer stands for Scholastic Achievement Test or even Scholastic Aptitude Test. The acronym doesn't stand for anything anymore—it's simply the most successful test in America run by the most successful test-makers in America. It doesn't have to stand for anything.

Building and running the SAT machine is a big job, and one that ETS ensures it is singularly capable of accomplishing. ETS and its largest client, College Board, have spent half of the last century striving to achieve two important benchmarks: reliability and validity. A test is reliable if it produces the same results over time. A test is valid if it accurately measures the skill or ability it purports to measure. The SAT has been trying to predict how a high school student will perform during his first year of college and has been trying to get consistent predictions over decades.

In order to claim that the SAT can make reliable and valid predictions, ETS has had to make sure of several things. First, that SAT scores are comparable from test to test—a student taking the May 2005 test should achieve approximately the same score as he would on the November 2006 test. This requires not just that each test is fungible with any other test, but that the test itself is standardized, so that each student in each test administration is measured with the same stable measuring rod. Second, that security and confidentiality be inviolate—no small feat for a standardized test with the vast range of administration of the SAT. Finally, ETS has to ensure that the SAT continues, despite years of alterations and criticisms ranging from racial bias to grammatical errors, to possess a reputation for testing intellectual aptitude rather than classroom achievement. In other words, people need to equate SAT scores with intelligence for the SAT to retain its position in the pedagogical world. Without this critical last factor, the SAT becomes a meaningless and arbitrary people-sorting machine, one that cannot claim to equalize the playing field of socioeconomically biased secondary school educations. America, and those parts of the world hoping to send their students to America, must believe that the SAT can find merit in the disadvantaged and undereducated and will reward that merit by opening the doors of elite universities. Overwhelmingly, ETS has met these goals in the SAT. People believe in the test, so it works.

While no one can argue the reliability of the SAT, barring scanning errors, its validity continues to be challenged. In fact, the substance and form of the SAT have changed several times over the past few decades. For the average consumer, however, actual validity is much less important than perceived validity. Most American families are content to let the universities battle ETS on the question of the SAT's validity while they focus instead on making sure their sons and daughters snag the highest score possible. And as long as universities continue to rely on the SAT, high school students will continue to take the SAT.

What all those statisticians spend their days doing in consultation with all those psychometricians and educational psychologists is making sure that their product keeps capturing the testing market. Like any good manufacturer, ETS needs to be indispensable to the college admissions process. So far, those statisticians and psychometricians have been right on the money: their product, the SAT, delivers a consistent and reliable ranking of millions of hopeful students year after year. Further, the SAT has withstood any number of attacks from students, parents, schools, and universities, seemingly without even slowing down production.

Every year the publication of SAT scores is met by intense scrutiny from parents, educators, and civil rights leaders. Schools and parents often look to SAT scores as a measurement of how well the schools are educating their children. Civil rights advocates and concerned citizens generally look at the disparity of scores between different racial and socioeconomic groups to see if the gaps are widening or closing. Scores trending in the wrong direction generate great consternation and further criticism of the SAT. Gone are the days of questionable analogies, such as "regatta: oarsman," that raised the ire of critics citing unfairness and bias. What inner-city child, after all, would have had occasion to come across a regatta? (Gone altogether, for that matter, are analogies.)

In 2005, the first year of the new SAT, criticism included a revelation of serious scoring mistakes by Pearsons, the firm contracted to score the test. This triggered a New York state senate hearing, headed by state senator Kenneth P. LaValle,[2] and a class action lawsuit brought by a Minnesota law firm on behalf of affected students.[3] If the media furor over the scoring snafu wasn't enough, the accumulation and analysis of statewide scores revealed that average scores on the SAT had dropped, reversing an otherwise positive trend for the decade as a whole.[4]

Critics can say what they want about ETS and the College Board—and there always seems to be a lot to say—but whatever it is that ETS is selling, people are buying. Every year's onslaught of lawsuits and attacks subsides as nervous high school juniors sharpen their pencils to take the SAT yet again. No matter the controversy or criticism, students will continue to take the test as long as colleges require it. As long as colleges require the SAT, students will believe that the test must be a reliable and accurate predictor of their academic worth.

What Is ETS Selling?

Your daughter may be relieved to hear that her biology test will be graded on a curve: if she bombs it, hopefully everyone else will too, and she'll be mercifully handed a respectable C. The SAT will always be graded on a curve, but that's not always good news to the examinees. All students who take the SAT are graded against each other rather than against a strict numerical scale. This is inherent to the basic purpose of standardized testing for college admissions: universities want the elite students, the top percentiles, not necessarily just the empirically well-prepared students. If, by some freak anomaly, almost all of the students taking the SAT answered almost all of the questions correctly, one might assume that ETS still pledges to rank those students on that eternal curve so that colleges can determine which students were infinitesimally better and thus more deserving of admission. What good is it to Harvard, after all, if *all* of its applicants sport perfect scores?

By the way, a perfect score is no longer 1600. The new SAT ushered in a whole new section, the writing test, with its own 800 possible points to add. With 800 math section points, 800 critical reading (the old verbal section), and 800 writing, a perfect score is now 2400. Remember, however, with the curve, that "perfect" isn't a fixed number of correct questions. With a bell curve, a student can miss several questions and still get a perfect score. Even more confusing, with that bell curve, a missed question in math may not count the same as a missed question in critical reading or writing. ETS will doctor the curve until the proportions of scores matches the curve.

The curve, therefore, can push nearly identical testers into artificial hierarchies. One misstep can drop an otherwise perfect tester down 20 or 30 points as the curve seeks to correct an errant bulge in scoring. Additionally, because scores are always multiples of ten, the gap between a 1790 student and an 1800 student can seem meaningful and can make a critical difference in college admissions. The benchmarks of scoring become harder to pin down when a student's score is not based strictly on the number of correct answers but on how others performed on that same test.

There's a lot of chatter about the increased difficulty of the SAT since the March 2005 "upgrade," which aimed to appease critics who claimed the test was outdated and ineffective, but the curved grading system assures that students will most often shuffle themselves out similarly regardless of test changes. If the same group of students takes a more difficult test, the statisticians predict that the top students will score at the top and the bottom students will score at the bottom, regardless of test difficulty. The curve makes sure of that. Difficulty, however, is not easy to measure, even on standardized tests. The SAT always has and always will test a specific and peculiar skill set, and altering the range of that skill set won't change that fact.

So why does the SAT matter for admissions? Who exactly is buying this bell curve, and why? The most cynical answer might be because of *U.S. News & World Report*. Arguably, few things have changed the college admissions landscape as much as the annual ranking of colleges by that zealous periodical. The rankings are based on several criteria, but all are numerical, and few are as difficult to argue with as the average high school GPA and average SAT score of enrolled freshmen. As an added bonus, those are two numbers that parents and prospective students understand very well.

GPA and SAT, incidentally, are the two variables of the college-ranking rubric that can be most directly affected by admissions decisions. Alumni giving, graduation rates, professor-to-student ratio—the other quantifiable variables are less affected by what happens during admissions committee meetings. So when a college weighs prospective students, it is always tempting to choose students with higher scores to boost its ranking. After all, a higher rank will result in more applications, a higher selectivity, and an overall increase in prestige.

In fact, *U.S. News & World Report* has started to wield an inordinate amount of power in the college ranking wars, so much so that some schools, such as Reed College in Portland, Oregon, have begun to opt out of the system entirely. For the vast majority who have chosen to stay and play the ranking game, jumping up just a few spots can make a critical difference in the popularity and prosperity of their schools, which makes paying close attention to SAT scores that much more attractive. Imagine a university attempting to increase its ranking in the annual *U.S. News & World Report* college issue. It's not so easy to increase the faculty-student ratio or decrease average class size or stimulate more generous alumni donations. You also would have a difficult time making quick or inexpensive changes to the various quality of life factors. You can, however, admit and matriculate students with higher SAT scores and jump up more easily in the rankings that way.

Additionally, the average SAT scores of students at school X, Y, or Z both affect and respond to consumer demand. If I am trying to decide between school X and Y for my son or daughter and think highly of both, it's hard not to think better of the one with an average SAT score 100 points higher. Schools that post high SAT scores are more attractive to other students with high SAT scores. It's like a club. Remember that despite much evidence to the contrary, there is a common perception that SAT scores serve as a reliable proxy for intelligence. Who doesn't want to go to the school where the smart kids go?

For a more practical and less conspiracy-driven analysis, imagine being an admissions official looking at thousands, if not tens of thousands, of applications. If you can use a combination of GPA and SAT scores to mathematically and automatically eliminate one-third to one-half of the applicants, you can now spend 50 to 100 percent more time looking at the remaining applicants and, arguably, make better decisions.

Moreover, as College Board studies attest and have generally been endorsed, GPA and SAT scores combined are a better indicator of first-year college success than is GPA alone. As loathed as the SAT is by so many, imagine trying to look simply at GPA. It would be a daunting challenge to compare my son's honors English class to your daughter's AP English class, particularly if my son's school doesn't offer AP classes. Or, in another scenario, what if my son's school is a tiny public high school that has had but a handful of applicants to college X in its entire history and your daughter's school is a tony private boarding school with a long history of sending its graduates to college X? It could be perilously easy to return to the very chummy situation that existed before the widespread use of the SAT when certain young men from certain schools were accepted to certain colleges simply because the heads of those schools in effect anointed those boys. The SAT was first championed by James B. Conant, then president of Harvard, to break that cozy relationship and broaden the pool of men from which the class was drawn.[5] (They didn't think of including women until some time later.)

However you look at it, schools simply don't always have the resources to do the kind of in-depth and nuanced application consideration that we all agree would be ideal. Moreover, without using numerical criteria, admissions officials would have to play the very fuzzy game of determining whose life experiences are more meaningful and which school's classes are more rigorous. While the SAT broke the hold of the elite private boarding schools on Ivy League admissions, it has brought its own slew of preferences and prejudices. To the point that American universities have bought into the utility of the bell curve, they've admitted a certain degree of defeat in the quest to ensure that the most qualified and able applicants are, in fact, the very students granted admission to their schools of choice. On the other hand, to the degree that American universities rely on the SAT to sort out the masses of applications landing on admissions desks across the country, they have set a reliable and consistent standard for prospective students. The SAT, and its bell curve, may not be every student's best friend, but it is far from fickle.

How Does ETS Do It?

For nearly 60 years, Educational Testing Service has been quietly gathering a staggering amount of quantitative and qualitative data about how students take the SAT.[4] As tutors, we explain to our students that ETS knows their reading lists in their English classes, which vocabulary workbooks they've been required to complete, and all the details of their mathematics curriculum. ETS knows not just what math skills most high school juniors have learned, but also the precise processes students use to solve problems. ETS has read the manuals for their calculators. From its inception, ETS has filled its advisory boards with educators and school administrators for just this reason. In short, ETS knows exactly what high school students know, and more importantly, what they don't know.

Even more critically, ETS knows how high school students approach tests, how they respond to stress and fatigue, and just which triggers are likely to cause the average high school student to jump to a false conclusion, misplace a decimal point, panic, or give up entirely. ETS knows how to create a test that challenges not just students' knowledge but their psyches as well. The biggest mistake we see students make is in underestimating the psychological toll the SAT can take. They prep for the questions, not for the test.

The pressure doesn't stop with the test itself. Every aspect of the testing experience has been crafted to create not just a substantive examination but a true test of endurance and psychological toughness. ETS tests the length of the test, the order of the sections, the individual questions, the order of the questions, and pretty much anything else you can think of. They're the experts, after all, and they do a thorough job. What is the result? A Saturday morning crowd of nervous, jumpy teenagers toting pencils, calculators, and IDs. Last-minute cramming, frantic searches for the correct room, and confusion everywhere. It's not just a test. It's the SAT experience.

What is truly remarkable is that this scene plays itself out in schools across America, and, to a lesser scale, in various cities around the world. And this now happens seven times a year and has been happening like this since the middle of the last century. To the extent that the SAT is about emotional reaction rather than solely quantitative evaluation, nothing has changed for decades. The SAT has evoked reliably panicked responses in a near-perfect progression for as long as any of us can remember and promises to continue to do so for as far as any of us can project.

And since the SAT is about emotional reaction rather than quantitative evaluation, and due to the superimposition of that trustworthy bell curve, the SAT continues to provide astonishingly reliable test results. Students fall into a scoring "rut," not because they lack the ability to select a greater number of correct answer choices, but because their learned responses to the psychological pathways on the test tend to remain steady.

You can read article after article propounding the opinion that the SAT is an invalid test, that its artificiality results in meaningless score assignments further impugned by racial bias, regional bias, and stereotype bias. It's not hard to find someone who firmly believes that the SAT doesn't test anything at all. What you won't find is any credible report that the SAT lacks reliability—because it doesn't. Whatever it is that the SAT tests, it coughs up the same reliable results, over and over again.

Why Do We Fall for It?

As anyone who has spent his professional life studying the SAT can tell you, it's a shockingly consistent test. Most of the tutors we work with make a habit of filing into an alphabetized seat in a high school classroom several times a year to keep a close watch on the test, and they regularly churn out perfect scores. Are we all geniuses? Born standardized testers? Not at all. Anyone who has seen and worked with that many SATs over the years could probably take the test in his sleep.

Once a student has tapped into the pattern that the SAT employs faithfully on each test, that student too can become an SAT genius. All the student has to do is become reasonably comfortable with the substantive material on the test and then employ that knowledge of the test and its content. That student will crush the test. So why doesn't this happen for most kids? Why doesn't consistent and steady practice always lead to perfect scores?

Just as the SAT employs certain patterns in its testing, so each test-taker reacts in patterned and habitual ways to the test. For most kids, the way they act and react on the SAT is informative not just of their typical testing behavior but of a lifetime of beliefs and experiences, educational and otherwise. We live and die by our habits, on the SAT and elsewhere. Altering a student's visceral response to the test may be more difficult than teaching him a thousand vocabulary words.

The creators of the SAT know all of this. They've hunted out those educational patterns and habits that plague our children. They've sorted out the mathematical habitual responses, the verbal beliefs and behaviors, and the test-taking routines that people have carried around with them since childhood. And, of course, they have used this information to build a test that consistently and successfully exploits the psychological abilities of examinees. It isn't enough to know all the vocabulary words: ETS is testing so much more than that.

Remember how much the makers of the SAT love the bell curve? Really, college admissions folks love the bell curve, and how useful it is in separating out the thousands and tens of thousands of applications colleges receive in growing numbers each year. Because of the historically huge crush of applicants, the SAT is now even more useful for sorting out the great seas of applications colleges receive yearly—1920 you're in; 1890 you're not. Now, admissions folks will say the SAT is just one tool (which it is) and that they don't have arbitrary cutoffs (which may be true). In the end, a standardized test is a somewhat blunt but effective tool for admissions committees. Arguably the most important criterion for them is that the scores are consistent, that my 620 on last June's test can reliably compare to your 700 on the January SAT or my friend's 590 on the May SAT. Moreover, admissions people are happy to continue to use the SAT only if my 620 is felt to be the same as a 620 last year and the year before that and the year before that and so on.

Getting those consistent scores on that beautifully stable bell curve year after year takes some real skill. Some would argue that it takes trickery. And here we get back to the math problem with which we started the chapter. Why do most people answer 5000 when the math is so easy to do? The key to that trick is what is known as conditioning, something well known to parents but less to students. We explain to our students that the test-makers know more about how students think than they themselves do. That's their job. Chances are you know who Pavlov is and all about his dogs, but in case you don't, here's a version to give your kids.

So this guy Pavlov was what is known as a behavioral psychologist. In his most famous experiment, he had all of these dogs in cages. Every day, he'd bring them food. But first, he'd ring a bell. Every day he'd ring that bell, walk to a shed, pull a can off the shelf, open it with a can opener, put the food in a bowl, walk around the shed, fumble with his keys, unlock the door, fill their water bowls, and finally give them the food. After days or weeks of hearing a bell and then getting fed, never one without the other, the dogs were conditioned. Mr. P could get up at 3 AM, trudge downstairs in his slippers to ring that bell, and the dogs would awake with anticipation. And there would be Sparky and Fido salivating like mad, thinking "Boy oh boy! Food!" Now, if they had really been thinking, they would have wondered, "Hey, why is it so dark? Are we really getting fed? Man, I could swear I can usually see my paws at dinnertime. What the heck is going on?" But, nope, there they were, slobbering all over themselves, thinking "Food! I heard the bell, so it must be dinnertime."

In school, teachers try to instill a process in their students. For years after you took geometry, when you heard "A squared plus B squared," you might add "equals C squared" despite the fact that your brain had lost track of all sense of the meaning or use of that formula. On tests, test-takers will fall in line with their own conditioning, working through questions the way they have been taught. You can be sure that the cadre of educational psychologists, statisticians, and psychometricians at ETS know those patterns. It's the key to generating that bell curve distribution of scores.

Consider for a moment how few kids get an 800 on the math part of the test. Now, consider how many kids get top grades in math, how many true math geeks there are in any school. Why don't they all get 800s on that section? Consider also that if the test-makers wanted a bell curve distribution, they would need only to extend the math content through calculus, letting the students fan themselves out over the bell curve according to the level of math course they had reached. ETS doesn't do that; the math content on the SAT covers arithmetic, algebra, and geometry. The advanced algebra content goes only through functions. It does not include trigonometry, precalculus, or calculus. That's 8th, 9th, and 10th grade math for most students and nothing beyond that. The SAT takes relatively mild subject matter and twists it in a way that makes questions difficult. Yes, one must know the underlying content, but it is the peculiar way the math is presented that makes it tricky.

For example, average, or arithmetic mean, is a math concept familiar to most students. Consider the Pavlovian conditioning of averages. In your mind, finding the average likely involves adding up specific numbers and dividing by the number of numbers. Take a look at Table 1.1 for a flashback on how most of us learned to do averages:

Table 1.1

Specific numbers	+ Add together	Sum	÷ Divide by number	Average
2, 4, 6	2 + 4 + 6	12	÷3	4
10, 15	10 + 15	25	÷2	12.5
15, 15, 17, 17	15+15+17+17	64	÷4	16

This process is so ingrained that the typical student will take any numbers given and follow suit regardless of what the question asks for. A typical, albeit easy, version of the way averages pop up on the SAT might look like this:

The average of 3 numbers is 12. What fourth number must be added so that the average of all four numbers is 15?

The typical test-taker is likely to immediately divide 12 by 3. After all, that's what averages are about, right? Well, the test-makers know that. To solve this, we must do just the opposite. If the average of 3 numbers is 12, then the sum of those 3 numbers is 36, or 12 times 3. The sum when the fourth number is added must be 60, as 4 x 15 = 60. So, if all four numbers add up to 60 and the first three numbers added up to 36, what must the fourth number be? 60 – 36 = 24. Not hard, just not what teens are conditioned to do when an averages question appears. Essentially, it's just the opposite, multiplying to get the sum and subtracting to get a specific number, rather than adding numbers and dividing to get the average.

Every competent math student feels capable of attacking a standard systems of equations problem, and the SAT obliges them. There is more than one way to solve these, however. ETS hopes to dupe you into doing it the way you were taught in school. For example:

If $8x - 3y = 11$ and $5x + 3y = 4$, find $3x - 6y$.

Our math teachers have taught us to solve for one variable, put that value back into an equation to find the other variable, and then put both variables in to find the answers. Like this:

$$
\begin{aligned}
8x - 3y &= 11 \\
\underline{5x + 3y = 4} \qquad &\text{(add the equations)} \\
13x + 0y &= 15
\end{aligned}
$$

$$13x = 15$$

$$x = \frac{15}{13}$$

$$\frac{8\,(15)}{13} - 3y = 11 \qquad \left(\text{plug in } \frac{15}{13} \text{ for } x\right)$$

$$\frac{120}{13} - 3y = 11$$

$$-3y = -\frac{120}{13} + 11$$

$$-3y = -\frac{120}{13} + 11\left(\frac{13}{13}\right)$$

$$-3y = -\frac{120}{13} + \frac{143}{13}$$

$$-3y = \frac{23}{13}$$

$$\left(-\frac{1}{3}\right)(-3y) = \frac{23}{13}\left(-\frac{1}{3}\right)$$

$$y = \frac{-23}{39}$$

$$\text{so, } 3x - 6y = 3\left(\frac{15}{13}\right) - 6\left(\frac{-23}{39}\right) \qquad \begin{array}{l}\text{(plug in the values} \\ \text{for } x \text{ and } y \text{ to} \\ \text{solve the equation)}\end{array}$$

$$= \frac{45}{13} + \frac{138}{39}$$

$$= \left(\frac{3}{3}\right)\left(\frac{45}{13}\right) + \frac{138}{39}$$

$$= \frac{135}{39} + \frac{138}{39}$$

$$= \frac{273}{39}$$

$$= 7$$

Ta-da! It's elegant, it's correct, and it took a whopping seven minutes of the precious 25 allotted to a math section.

Now, I tell my students, the kind folks at ETS are a bunch of smarty-pants and love to remind themselves of this. They design problems so that if only you were slick like they think they are, you could avoid the above mess. The trick is to *pay close attention to what you are trying to find.* There is always a shortcut. The best way to solve these problems is a way most students weren't taught in school: write one equation on top of the other and then see how to match them up.

$$8x - 3y = 11$$
$$5x + 3y = 4$$

How do we get to 3x – 6y? Don't think of having one part canceling another, but rather pay attention to the first coefficients, 8 and 5. How do we get 3x? We subtract.

$$8x - 3y = 11$$
$$- (5x + 3y = 4)$$

$$8x - 3y = 11$$
$$\underline{- 5x - 3y = -4}$$
$$3x - 6y = 7$$

Our work is done.

Now, imagine the above under pressure. With the pressure of time and anxiety, any test-taker is that much more likely to take the SAT in ways that play into the designs of the test-makers.

One of the most deeply ingrained reactions is the perceived need to answer every question on the test. That is, after all, the *modus operandi* of pretty much any good student on any test. Leaving questions blank on an academic test is likely a recipe for disaster. Skipped 10 percent altogether? Well, there goes that A. Sigh. But on the SAT, answering 90 percent of the questions correctly and skipping 10 percent can yield scores in the 700s. Not too bad. It's just that the "need" to do all of the questions likely has more to do with conditioned responses and students' comfort zones than the reality of the SAT. But, students don't know that. Even if they did, knowing that is the case and actually adjusting accordingly are very different things.

ETS is good at what it does. If my score accurately measures my ability, well, that's great for me. If not, that's still great for ETS.

***

So what is the secret of the 5000/4100 trick? It involves conditioning and a peculiarity of the human brain deemed the "magic number 7." Taking the latter part first, the human brain seems to be comfortable with holding on to up to 7 pieces of information. Holding more than that becomes harder. Consider that phone numbers are 7-digit numbers. The first part, the conditioning, involves the way that we chunk up information for our memories. That 7-digit phone number is easy to remember in chunks of three or four digits each, as long as it follows a familiar pattern. Try memorizing this number: 180-05-5-512-12. A little tricky to keep in your mind, right? Now try this one: 1-800-555-1212. Not so bad that way, is it?

The 5000/4100 trick is based on 8 numbers and a pattern. It pushes your memory past its 7-number limit, and gets your mind established in a pattern. It goes back and forth from the 1000s digit to the 10s digit so that when you get to 4090 and add 10, your brain has been set up to roll back to the 1000s digit. For most people, it does, "completing" the 90 with a 10 and getting 5000 rather than the correct 4100. If you present this trick orally rather than on paper, you can control the pace, adding both anxiety and the pressure of time. With a little bit of knowledge of how most people's minds work most of the time, a little conditioning and a little pressure, it's possible to almost guarantee the results you want.

***

The educational psychologists study students, what they know and do not know, the processes they have been taught, and the conditioning they have absorbed. By employing some tricks and inducing anxiety, they generate a bell curve distribution of scores that would make any statistician proud.

What can you do about this? To a certain extent, sustained practice with actual SAT questions grants a student a fairly good view of his erroneous testing patterns. Seeing your own patterns can be hard, however, and not defending your own patterns is usually even harder. The exact extent of the helpfulness of this method depends on the nature and depth of the student's testing "mannerisms." When issues of self-concept and anxiety fold into taking the SAT, as they too often do, practice becomes more frustration than edification. Some habits of testing require more than repetition to root out, as repetition tends to solidify habit rather than to illuminate error.

Throughout the remainder of this book, we'll discuss ways to positively shape a student's response to the test. When your son overcomes his negative test-taking habits or your daughter conquers crippling anxiety, the individual test questions won't seem daunting at all. Anyone can teach your child a few math tricks and some reading strategies, but helping your student become a successful test-taker and adult just may fall to you.

HOW DO WE CONQUER THIS TEST?

I tutored a bright teenager named Ryan, who seemed apathetic about his mediocre scores. I knew he was sharp enough to score higher, but I couldn't seem to make him care enough to get the job done. As I talked more with Ryan, I learned more and more about his lacrosse team, his games, and his position on the field. It dawned on me that this was a competitive kid when you got him out on the playing field. When it came to the SAT, he just hadn't heard that there was a game going on.

I started talking to Ryan about ETS, who they were, and what they were doing. I showed him how simple math problems were presented in complex and confusing ways. I explained how ETS needed to make smart kids trip up in order to keep the score allocation even. Ryan started to get mad.

We looked at the organization of the test and how kids get tricked into spending valuable time working on problems that they'll never get correct anyway. We looked at the length of the test, and how kids start to wither in energy and accuracy at the end, pulling down their combined scores. Ryan was really angry now.

As soon as Ryan learned who his enemy was, he buckled down. Face to face with a challenge, Ryan knew how to win. It wasn't easy, but that was fine by Ryan. When he finally saw the test for what it was, a light went on.

"This test really sucks!" he exclaimed.

"Yes, it does," I allowed, "but it sucks consistently."

Ryan took advantage of that consistency to figure out his opponent's weaknesses and to learn how to take advantage of them. He relished the challenge of a practice test and reveled in his minor victories. When test day finally came, he beat the test and loved every minute of it.

Lambasting standardized tests has become a preoccupation for many, and an occupation for some, and it may be that their point of view is worth considering. Hating the test won't help your child on the day of the SAT, however. What will help is an understanding of the basic nature of the SAT, and how your teenager can take advantage of that consistent basic nature to keep from being outsmarted by the exam.

Universities need a reliable measuring stick, and ETS provides that to them. Test after test pushes the same psychological buttons on student after student. Children can learn to break free from the routine by finally unearthing the buried machinations of the SAT and altering their response to them.

What is test-taking, after all, but responding to stimuli? So much of the SAT experience is emotional response, rather than rational response, and as such the average teen cannot hope to beat out a test built by some of the most skilled practitioners in the art of understanding how teenagers think. Simply put, ETS knows exactly what it's doing, and until your students do as well, they won't have a hope of besting the best test-makers out there.

As students become more aware of the emotional drivers controlling their testing behavior, they can learn to tweak or redirect those drivers into positive responses and habits. Rather than feeling defeated and demoralized by a difficult sentence completion question, they can recognize that trigger and build a habit of responding differently. Instead of madly rushing through a math section, bent on total completion and resulting in slipshod work, students can take charge of their timing and work in a measured and more accurate fashion, no longer slave to an unforgiving timer.

The fact is that most students have the ability to learn enough information to answer most of the SAT questions correctly. Take away the oppressive proctor, the mind-numbing instructions and paperwork, and the relentless ticking of the clock, and you'll really see what your kids can do. While you can't create an external environment to aid your daughter's and son's scoring potential, you can help them change their responses to the environment they must work in. They can learn successful strategies that create a confidence and assurance strong enough to ward off the worst anxiety, panic, and discouragement.

PARENTS HAVE HABITS TOO

At first blush, the SAT appears to be solely the province of teenagers. Indeed, as parents, we're highly unlikely to accept blame if our kid's scores plummet, but we may well be inclined to flaunt a top score earned by our son or daughter. And it's true that during those 3 hours and 45 minutes we can't be in the testing room with our kids, and we can't rescue a drowning score. But to claim that we have nothing to do with those scores is to deny the central role many of us already play in our kids' testing angst as well as in their successes.

One of the ways in which we impact our kids long before they ever register to take the SAT is through our own patterns and habits of behavior. Our kids not only watch us deal with our own challenges through our predictable, patterned responses, but they also, consciously or not, model their own behaviors after the examples they see in such close proximity. To an extent, the way our kids deal with stresses and challenges is either an imitation or a reaction to our own patterns of behavior.

A critical, often overlooked piece of this puzzle is the pattern of our interactions with our children. It can be hard to imagine how our personal relationship with our children can affect a standardized test score, but we'll discuss that issue in more depth in the following pages. For now, it's worth noting that the test is affecting *your* life as well as your teen's. You're taking the time to read this book, after all. For many parents, their involvement is simply the desire to help their children in the beastly struggle that the SAT and college admissions procedures have become. For others, the SAT will evoke memories and emotions from long ago, some part of which may influence your child's present experience.

As a parent, you'll have a much better chance of guiding your child through the labyrinths of later high school and college preparation if you are aware of not only the complex issues that can arise, but of your own and your child's responses to those issues. When we acknowledge the SAT for the emotional and psychological gauntlet it so often turns out to be, we are better prepared to navigate the test successfully, emotions and family relations intact. The families who are aware of, informed about, and engaged in this process emerge not only with the desired college acceptance letters in hand, but with strengthened relationships, and more confident and capable young adults ready to begin their promising university careers.

CHAPTER TWO

Clobbering the Critical Reading

After the initial buzz about a harder math section and the new (gasp!) essay, the real change in the new SAT is in the sheer volume of reading passages. Suddenly, kids who could fudge their way through a few passages are finding themselves slammed into an interminable wall of words, a good percentage of which they've never seen before. The old SAT was about reading comprehension; the new SAT is about reading endurance.

How long is it? Let's put it this way: the new SAT that was unveiled in March 2005 is fully 45 minutes longer than the old SAT. This additional time is the typical length of a high school test in its entirety, making the new SAT a total of 3 hours and 45 minutes. That's without breaks, without proctor instructions, and without the 30 to 45 minutes required for assigning seats and filling in bubble sheets. When over a third of that time is spent in three to four critical reading sections, you've got a lot of reading.

The amount of reading isn't the only challenge. The passages themselves are more difficult. They're denser and riddled with college-level vocabulary words. How hard are the words? Here's a sampling: *maudlin, epicanthic, nebulous, demythologizing, opprobrium, surreptitious, aesthetician, anomalous, filial, anticoagulant, diminution, tarboosh, libertinism.* The SAT sometimes seems to specialize in arcane usages and agricultural vocabulary, just the words modern children of the cities and suburbs are likely never to have run across. A favorite ploy on the SAT is to play on the differences between the primary definition of a word and its secondary use, which is often the more commonly heard. What modern citizen equates *chauvinism* with fanatical patriotism rather than a belief in male superiority? And your kids? Try to explain *qualify* as meaning "to limit or restrict" and you'd think you had just suggested that an idol is really a false god rather than a gyrating singer.

And what about the phrases? *Causality violation, deterministic universe, sentimental intervention, environmental popularizers, auditory inwardness, physical economy.* In these cases, even if the student happens to know what the words themselves mean, she may find it nearly impossible to determine what their combinations signify. On top of this, it's not enough to figure out what the words and phrases mean—you have to be able to answer questions about them, too.

ETS is also fully aware that people, especially teens, tend to use language imprecisely. English, after all, is an ever-changing landscape—except on the SAT. We get away with subtly altering word definitions in conversation because we rely on context, nuance, phrasing, body language, and our specific relationships with the people with whom we converse. The SAT, however, is so precise in its word usage that it focuses on the principal definitions of words and seems to teenagers to give other meanings to words they commonly use differently.

Take the word *unique*. Many people misuse this word to mean "unusual" or even "quirky." A reasonable guess on a critical reading question that uses "unusual" as a descriptor would actually be incorrect because something unique must be one of a kind. What about the word *anxious*? Students tell me all the time that they are anxious for summer, for the sweet sixteen party this weekend, for the prom. "What's to worry about?" I question, and they respond with confusion. *Anxious* comes from *anxiety*, and technically does not refer to positive excitement or anticipation. The SAT makes full use of this kind of misunderstanding.

It's going to take a little while for colleges and other educational professionals to realize that capable kids are routinely underperforming on this test. After all, education has always been about literacy, so why shouldn't we test that? Our high school students read all the time, for almost every class. What's the big deal? Why are kids underachieving on such a familiar task set?

There are several answers to these questions. Vocabulary is a big one, and we'll discuss that in some detail. Next is reading differences and learning disabilities. Many kids have not been forced to read at the length and pace that the SAT requires, and are unable to instantly adapt to the demands of the new test. Adding to the challenge of the sheer bulk of reading is the fact that virtually no teenager I've ever met is even faintly interested in the subject matter of SAT reading passages. When you add exhaustion and low confidence to the list, the critical reading sections become quite a challenge indeed, but a challenge that, with the right skills and attitude, can be overcome by just about anyone.

***

Meeting Joe

Joe was the star athlete son of intellectual parents, accountants at the top of their games. Joe was a straight-A student but unabashedly and self-avowedly not *an intellectual. He worked hard for his top grades, bringing to his studies the same drive and breathtaking tenacity that made him succeed in sports. Of average size and build, Joe was beloved by his teachers and coaches for his strong work ethic. A lifelong fan and player of baseball and basketball, Joe had been made captain of his basketball team in his junior year, beating out more talented seniors because he brought to practice each day the focus and energy the upperclassmen lacked. He joined cross-country that same year to be in better shape for basketball and quickly became the number two runner on the team, based mainly on grit and his stubborn refusal to lose.*

His mom approached me after the return of his sophomore PSAT scores, declaring with alarm, "Joe's never going to be able to go to college!" Joe, like so many of the athletic teenage boys I've seen, didn't enjoy reading. His vocabulary was weak, particularly given his straight A's and the scores he'd need for the schools he and his parents had their sights set on. However, Joe dutifully read what he was assigned in school. His parents had always seen to that. By the time I met him, working hard was as instilled in Joe as if he'd been born running and never stopped.

THE VOCABULARY OF SUCCESS

We'll use Joe to discuss just why the SAT is such a challenging reading task. Remember, one of Joe's big challenges was his relatively low level of vocabulary. He didn't realize just how much that would affect his SAT score. Knowing every word on the SAT doesn't guarantee success, but it sure helps. Imagine taking the SAT in a foreign language. Though most of us have studied other languages, and might even feel fairly conversant in them, imagine trying to take the SAT in, say, Russian. When you don't feel comfortable with all the words, performing tasks such as answering questions about tone and drawing inferences can feel Herculean.

This situation is what many people, and many high school students, face daily. Though literate, many words are still "foreign" to them. But we all have ways around this. In conversation, we pick up on body language, tone, and expressions to glean the essential meaning. Or we nod and smile appreciatively even when we don't understand, or we copy concern when a speaker's face shows distress. Moreover, most speakers purposefully choose words they believe we'll understand. After all, they usually want to be understood.

Written words are different. Authors cannot know who will pick up their books. They may hope they are writing for a highly literate and literary audience but find that the book becomes a favorite of 7th grade English teachers whose students have different abilities. There are also fewer opportunities to use tone to clarify word meaning.

So, when I read a passage in a book and don't understand a word, what do I do? A typical reaction is to stop, really look at the word, and see if I do in fact know it upon closer inspection. Do I know the root? Does it sound close to some other word I know? Is it simply a different part of speech of a familiar word? If unmet by success, I will reread the sentence looking for the basic meaning, perhaps rereading the previous or following sentence or sentences. If I think the word is significant or I'm really stumped by its meaning, I turn to the dictionary. Then, I continue on, hoping I've not missed anything essential or lost the train of the meaning in the passage.

Arguably, the essential meaning of a text or even a paragraph won't hinge on one word. But it might. And even if it doesn't, consider what happens if the above description is played out repeatedly through a paragraph or passage. Texts that are wholly coherent to the author and most writers may begin to look like the swiss cheese that top-secret documents released for the public resemble when they've had word after word, phrases, and entire sentences blacked out by an overly zealous censor. It becomes likely that essential information is lost. Even if it's not, the process of retracing your steps while reading is slow. It's frustrating and it's tiring—all factors that add up to an unsuccessful reading experience. For Joe, it added up to a sustained dislike for reading and SAT scores well below his potential.

Take a look at the following as an example. This is a typical, if fairly easy, example of a paragraph that you might find in an SAT reading passage. The new SAT contains passages much more difficult and dense. First the paragraph is presented as a typical high school student with a low- to mid-level vocabulary would read it:

> The uitdagendig gezilleg statement that the Guggenheim makes is toch more lekker than it is ausgezijgend. The entire north of Spain, from Santander in the west to the ruw Pyrenees in the east, has kruispunt with an jeugdherberg toevloed of tourists over the past three years. Although enkele planners vertrekt early oosten of 500,000 visitors per year, after the first eight months, nearly 700,000 bezienswaardigheden had heft met open monden gehorlogt in begrijp at Mr. Gehry's work. Aside from bringing iemand and alstublieft opbrengsten into Bilbao, the Guggenheim gekatalyseerd the city's enkele retourtje program. The hoeveel Guggenheim and the erheen infrastructuur have thus teamed up to help Bilbao capture a graag gedaan role in the aangenam European ausgezijgend.

Not only is this gobbledygook, but it probably took a little while to figure that out. "Wait a minute," you're saying, "that's not even all in English. How am I supposed to understand what it's saying, much less answer questions about it?" Pretty discouraging, right? And, reading something when you don't know the words can add to the sense that "Gosh, I really am not good at this."

Now, let's say you have an average vocabulary level for a high school junior. This is what the passage looks like to you:

> The uitdagendig independent statement that the Guggenheim makes is arguably more economic than it is political. The entire north of Spain, from Santander in the west to the ruw Pyrenees in the east, has kruispunt with an incredible toevloed

of tourists over the past three years. Although urban planners vertrekt early estimates of 500,000 visitors per year, after the first eight months, nearly 700,000 bezienswaardigheden had heft in awe at Mr. Gehry's work. Aside from bringing immediate and significant opbrengsten into Bilbao, the Guggenheim gekatalyseerd the city's urban renewal program. The hoeveel Guggenheim and the graceful infrastructuur have thus teamed up to help Bilbao capture a significant economic role in the expanding European economy.

It's readable, and mostly understandable, but it takes you a bit of time to get through it. Answering comprehension questions will involve some detective work, and some of the questions will deal with the portions of the passage that you didn't quite understand.

Finally, here is the passage in its entirety, as someone who understands all of its words would read it:

The defiantly independent statement that the Guggenheim makes is arguably more economic than it is political. The entire north of Spain, from Santander in the west to the rugged Pyrenees in the east, has flourished with an incredible influx of tourists over the past three years. Although urban planners derided early estimates of 500,000 visitors per year, after the first eight months, nearly 700,000 *turistas* had gaped in awe at Mr. Gehry's work. Aside from bringing immediate and significant revenues into Bilbao, the Guggenheim catalyzed the city's urban renewal program. The acrobatic Guggenheim and the graceful infrastructure have thus teamed up to help Bilbao capture a significant economic role in the expanding European economy.

If you think the above paragraphs overstate the case, you haven't sat through preparation for the SAT like we have. Reading this version of the passage would give you a lot more confidence going into those reading comprehension questions. The more words a student knows, the more quickly he can move through the reading passages, and the more accurately he can answer the questions. Additionally and importantly, the more words a student knows and the more efficiently and accurately he can work through the critical reading sections, the more confidence and momentum he is able to sustain throughout the test. For Joe, overcoming his vocabulary problem was critical to keeping his confidence level high so that his struggles with words didn't also drag down his math score.

The solution to this vocabulary problem is just plain hard work. You've just got to know the words. Students come in convinced that because they didn't start reading *Little House on the Prairie* at age four, it's too late. If only he'd studied Latin, parents lament, this wouldn't be an issue. But this is an English test. With deference due Latin teachers everywhere, there is no substitute for knowing the precise meanings of words in English. The reality is that, yes, it would be great if your son spent all his summers with J.R.R. Tolkien instead of video games, but it's not too late now. Starting in the fall of junior year, learning just 25 vocabulary words a week gives you 1,000 new words before the SAT. That's a lot of new words.

Now, what are the odds that one of your new words will be *the word* that the hardest sentence completion question is looking for? My answer to students is to not worry about that sort of thing. We're not hoping to guess which words will be directly asked on the test. We're planning to have a broader base of vocabulary so that students will know all of the background words that are only indirectly tested. They will then be able to read the passages more quickly, understand the questions that are being asked, and eliminate incorrect answers on the sentence completions. ETS will always find a word that almost no one has ever heard of to test on the sentence completions. The prepared student, even if he doesn't know that word, will be able to eliminate the four other choices. Know four out of five words and you're set. Know three out of five and you'd better be lucky.

READING DIFFERENTLY

Vocabulary is not the only culprit for reading problems. Learning differences, from minor reading quirks to severe disabilities, account for many more. Critical reading is the section most likely to challenge the struggling reader with its endless passages about raven social behavior and scientific classification systems that require sustained concentration and quick processing. In fact, everything from processing disorders to an overly careful reading style affects the way students approach and deal with such tasks as memorizing vocabulary, organizing information, and making inferences from a set of facts.

Shouldn't they be learning how to improve on these tasks in school? My students tell me that it's not so difficult to go through high school without actually having to read anything other than CliffsNotes and someone else's class notes before the test. Some of these students who were diagnosed with a learning difference way back in middle school are using evasive techniques to get around their difficulties. In other words, they're not really learning how to read effectively. They're learning how to dodge reading assignments. That will get you through high school, perhaps, but the SAT is not as easy to manipulate. Some of these students are finding that even with extra time, even with medication, they simply cannot barrel their way through the SAT successfully.

Additionally, some of these students have been told their whole lives that they have a learning difference and perhaps have been treated differently because of that fact. Now they're shown the SAT and told to suck it up and get a good score. This combination of conflicting messages is likely to result in lower self-confidence for students who have been told that they need more time to do what other kids can do quickly. Even with extra time on the SAT (and not all kids with learning differences qualify for that, or are able to successfully convince ETS to grant that accommodation), it's tougher to have a competitive attitude when you don't feel equal to the task.

It can be difficult to tell when your child simply dislikes reading and when your child has an actual reading problem. Most people who fit one of those categories also fit the other. Reading dysfunction can manifest itself at a very early age in a child and often leads to a lifetime of avoiding reading, thereby compounding the problem. What so often happens is that a child has some difficulty with the mechanics of reading and therefore develops both an aversion to reading and a self-concept of being a bad reader. Research indicates that most people's academic self-concepts can be traced back to which first grade reading group they were assigned to.[1] If a child finds reading difficult and therefore unpleasant, the child will avoid it as much as possible, ensuring that reading skills remain underdeveloped, or unused and prone to rustiness. By the time that child hits high school, it can be difficult to tell what is the cause and what is the effect.

When we tutor these kids for the SAT, we often find teens who may have developed coping mechanisms for childhood dyslexia or have outgrown visual motor skill problems, but who possess a vocabulary several grade levels below where it should be. Having hated reading for so long and avoided it so assiduously, now they couldn't possibly tell you what "assiduously" means. They have a tremendous gulf of knowledge to cross before they can start to work on their actual reading skill sets.

The top reading specialist in our area spends quite a bit of time basically torturing her students with vocabulary, knowing that if people fundamentally don't know hundreds and hundreds of words, they can't get the meaning out of the sentences and paragraphs of text they are trying to read. Simply sounding out unfamiliar words isn't reading; to a large extent reading consists of recognition of meaning arranged in word and phrase form.

In addition, not knowing words, or even not easily and quickly recognizing words, slows readers down. This makes reading and doing homework unpleasant, but also obviously has ramifications for taking timed reading tests. Many people who have very good verbal reasoning skills learn to work around the words they don't know by reading in context. That sounds great in principle, but in practice this requires backing up and rereading sentences or parts of sentences in order to figure out what the unknown word likely means.

Students can, and do, spend precious time attempting to decipher the unfamiliar words, looking for root forms or digging through memory banks. Rather than quickly admitting defeat, as they'd have to if the words were actually blacked out, they continue to sound out the words and try to puzzle out meaning, all while the clock is ticking. Adding to that frustration, and remembering the student's fundamental and long-standing dislike of reading, the SAT becomes a hateful task indeed.

If you suspect that your child has a fundamental issue with reading, now is a great time to seek expert help. The SAT may help you catch a condition that has been sabotaging your child's best efforts for years. Your child may have worked around a reading difficulty in classroom academic work, but a timed standardized test is hard to outwit. Overcoming a reading difficulty will be beneficial on the SAT, but *crucial* for your child's academic and life success.

Trying to get a nonreader to read anything is important. Resist the temptation to force books down your child's throat, however. Remember, we're trying to overcome a combination of reading difficulty and reading dislike, and success on either of those axes will translate to ultimate success on both. Encourage your child to read anything, whether it's the newspaper or magazines or books.

Many times, kids and parents have the impression that only certain sorts of reading materials constitute "real" reading. Parents of teenage boys may despair that their kids consistently shun classic literature, not understanding that boys, statistically, much prefer nonfiction.[2] On the other side, parents of teenage girls often don't realize that the tweenie novelettes their daughters are devouring are helping to build a comfort level and ease in reading skills, even if not an immediately impressive vocabulary.

I often encourage students to find magazines about topics that interest them. Look for the *New Yorker* equivalent of your magazine of choice—magazines with sophisticated writing levels. For instance, try *Rolling Stone* rather than *People* magazine. Many teenagers can read sports magazines straight through, but can't manage to wade through any other text. Consider sportswriter John Feinstein's books. Moreover, if there is any book that your son or daughter has really liked, type the title into Amazon.com and you'll get lists of similar books for your child to try.

If students are really averse to reading in their leisure time and aren't likely to improve their vocabulary that way, try to make daily vocabulary part of an ongoing plan. You'd be surprised what 25 words a week will do for your child's confidence, skill, and enjoyment of reading. Helping your child to become a more adept reader may be one of the most important things you can do. After all, no matter what happens on the SAT, a solid vocabulary and some fundamental reading skills will serve your child well in college and beyond.

NOT ANOTHER BORING SAT PASSAGE!

Another culprit for poor performance in critical reading is lack of interest. I ask my students to describe how they read Harry Potter books, or *The Sisterhood of the Traveling Pants*, and many of them shriek out, "Oh, those books are so good! I read the sixth one in *two days!*" Now, a student who plods sluglike through reading passages about the Upper Ganges, complaining all the while, has just claimed to have read over 700 pages over a two-day period. How is this possible?

Books aimed at a teenage audience often use words that teenagers are familiar with (and in a familiar style—lots of slang and not a lot of punctuation and syntactic complexity) and focus on topics they are interested in. SAT reading passages, however, are rarely even faintly interesting to the average eleventh grader. And don't think that doesn't make a difference. Students, like adults, read more slowly when they aren't interested in what they're reading. They just do.

Some students overcome this through sheer adrenaline. Spooked by the time limits and the prospect of failing, they barrel through the reading passages in record time. Others, no matter how hard they want to, simply can't do this. It takes practice to read boring passages quickly, and many students have never had reason to practice.

Well, now there's a reason, and practice they must. My students find that the more passages they try, the better able they are to focus and read quickly. The reason for this is twofold. First, reading is a skill that improves with practice, and reading quickly and with exaggerated focus is no different. Second, the more reading passages students plow through, the more they understand how SAT reading passages work. They see more easily what the questions are looking for and are able to focus on those aspects of the passage that ETS is most likely to test. It becomes less of a reading exercise or reading skill, and more of a testing skill. Their focus is now not on the Upper Ganges but on outsmarting ETS, and that's actually pretty interesting if you think about it.

For Joe, facing the SAT reading passages as if he was facing an enemy was the key to engaging his interest. He was used to competition and knew how to push himself—both skills proved crucial in his struggle to pull his reading score up to where he thought it should be, and, in fact, where it could be. He started to read with a purpose: not necessarily to understand raven social behavior, which he wasn't apt to do no matter how carefully he read, but to get the information he needed to answer the questions he knew would follow. With that as his purpose, he found the passage much more interesting.

CONFIDENCE ISSUES

While confidence is an issue that affects nearly every aspect of the SAT, from anxiety management to skipping strategies, its role in reading success is too significant to ignore. The SAT triggers students' core self-concepts in two major areas: reading and math. For math, most students trace their beliefs about their abilities to either their algebra or their geometry class. If either went poorly, they feel labeled as "bad at math" from then on.

Self-concepts about reading originate earlier. From elementary school, all children know which reading group they belong to, and therefore whether or not they are "good readers." Think of the rigid demarcations often seen in fourth grade classrooms—the A group reads thick story books, while the B group has thinner ones, and the C group leaves the classroom for remedial aid. The process continues throughout elementary school and into middle school, where often students are grouped into classes by level of reading ability. That's a lot of years of reinforcement, which can be difficult to overcome.

Attacking the technical skills first can indirectly help to overcome this obstacle. As vocabulary improves, reading goes more quickly. Practice may not make perfect in this case, but it can show students that they are capable of making progress. Just shaking the foundation of self-doubt a bit is often enough to let students see that perhaps they're better readers than they thought. Confidence, so often, presents a chicken-and-egg conundrum—show a child that she is capable, and she will become so.

Joe's Story Continued

Joe put his mind to furiously learning words. A bright kid, words were simply hurdles to him. In his real life, he was a runner, but he ran cross-country—think open fields, let me fly! In learning words, he was systematically removing obstacles so he could fly through the reading passages. He was getting better, faster, and, most importantly, ever more confident.

In the early part of the season, Joe beat the top runner at a local school. This boy, his running nemesis as Joe's mom would have it, had always prevailed over Joe and his teammates. In late September, Joe beat him. Now the boy may have had a bad day, been sick, or stumbled. Who knows? What mattered was that Joe knew it was possible to beat him. And that made all the difference. In Joe's mind, he now "owned" this other runner. Belief was all he needed to make that final push, and Joe never lost to that runner again. Joe needed to know that he could similarly "own" the SAT, and that would be all it would take to declare victory.

In Joe's SAT preparation, he was always terrific at math, with his scores incrementally rising from low 600s to high 600s and then creeping just over 700. His verbal score (the reading section on today's SAT) was everyone's concern. Joe and his mom both knew that Joe was bright, but again, not an intellectual. It seems they feared one needed to be bookish and geeky to do well on the verbal section of the SAT. Certainly it helps to have read the entire English canon by age 16, but that was not the clay we were molding. Joe learned how to approach the reading systematically, how to see the passages and questions more from the perspective of the test-makers than through the eyes of a high school English student. And, he progressively improved.

One day, on one section of a practice test, Joe got a passage that just clicked. Arguably, it wasn't a terribly difficult or literary passage, but he clobbered it. Beaming, I told him that if he kept up that pace, we would "show his mom!" (He and I are both more than a little competitive and we relished the opportunity to tell his mom, "told you so!") At the end of that session, when his mom asked how he'd done, I explained that he'd done very well. Facing her, knowing Joe was just behind my right shoulder, I explained that were he to keep up the pace, he could score a 700 on the verbal portion of the SAT. Seeing her reaction was one of the most satisfying events of my life. Her eyes welled with tears and she covered her mouth, squeaking out a barely audible "Really?" I assured her he could.

And that made all the difference. Joe now knew he could do it. The SAT was now an opponent that he had already beaten, if only in pieces, and one he knew he could chase down to finish the job. And, not too surprisingly, he did just that.

CHAPTER THREE

Mutilating the Math Section

If I had a coin for every student I've tutored who said flat-out at our first meeting, "I'm bad at math," and if half of those coins were quarters, 200 were nickels, and the remaining one-sixth were dimes, how much money would I have? Well, the fact is, I'd have $95, but how many of you actually wanted to try to figure that out? And if you looked at that problem and felt confused, does that make you "bad at math"?

The first, and often greatest, hurdle to success on the math portion of the SAT is the endemic belief among high school students that 95 percent of people are "bad at math," and that only the remaining 5 percent, the hopelessly geeky, will ever be able to be successful on the math portion of the SAT. Except that they would probably never use percentages to express that belief. Through some bizarre demographic phenomenon, it seems that each high school in America was allotted at least one truly, horrifically bad math teacher. Every child who passed through the gauntlet of the class presided over by that terrible teacher and who wasn't enough of a math geek to "get it" in spite of the teacher will forever believe himself "bad" at either geometry or algebra. Sometimes it seems that there is no possible way to persuade these students that their plight is reversible.

It may be that the only way to overcome this formidable obstacle is to convince these disadvantaged children that the math section of the SAT is not, in actuality, about math. Here's the proof for those stubborn students who insist on focusing on all the numbers and symbols the section contains: Almost all of the formulas that you need to work any problem in the math section are provided for you at the beginning of each section. In fact, you can bring your calculator, and you can program into it any formulas or equations you want. No calculating, no remembering formulas—what is the math section about? There it is: ETS does not care if you ever paid attention in math class. Seemingly, ETS is not interested in your math skills or in how bad you felt your algebra teacher was.

So why are there so many questions on this test that look convincingly like your daughter's last math test? Well, math is a nice way to test quantitative skills in a way that doesn't overly punish non-native English speakers, the way the other two sections do. Oddly enough, the math and verbal sections of the SAT test almost the very same thing: logical thinking, following directions, reading carefully, and working quickly. Not one student has ever walked into my office and announced, "I'm bad at following directions."

The refreshing thing about taking a quantitative-based test that is *not* interested in math skills is that any method that gets you to the answer is fair game. In fact, the test is constructed in such a way as to reward those students who skip steps, who search for shortcuts, and who use sneaky tricks to find the answer. The test can actually punish the careful students who feel concern for process and orderliness. The truly diabolical thing about the math section of the SAT is that even that 5 percent of kids who know that they are good at math won't necessarily ace this test. Again, it's not really about the math.

And that's the second barrier to success on the math test. After this besieged student has managed to cast off his former image of himself as "bad at math," he must then break down any beliefs he has about process integrity and instead learn to scramble greedily for answers in any fashion whatsoever, short of actually cheating. This often requires overcoming years and years of careful mathematics training and defying that particularly fierce geometry teacher who always made you show your work, or you didn't get full credit. The SAT never makes you show your work, and there is no partial credit.

This is the core of underperformance on the math section of the SAT: Every student who walks into the testing room on test day carries with him a set of beliefs about himself and math. Some of those beliefs will stand in the way of success by triggering anxiety, by prompting the student to work in unproductive ways, and by keeping up a steady stream of unhelpful self-talk. The math section of the SAT, more than any other section, is an exercise in suspending beliefs.

So much of math in school is about processes. We learn the rules of order of operations in arithmetic, needing these skills for a solid foundation in algebra I. If we don't get the core of algebra under our belts, we will likely founder in geometry, algebra II, trigonometry, and so on. Math teachers justifiably are like old grammar school teachers, chiding and imploring their students that process matters. Like instilling good technique in a tennis swing or piano playing, having solid processes can be key to carrying us from one level of math to the next.

The problems that this presents are twofold. One, we may have those processes so ingrained in us that derailing them is scary. We may feel adrift without them or have veritable flashbacks to being slammed on a test or called out in class for doing the problem the incorrect way. "No! No! No!" we may hear in our heads, "That's not the right way to do it!" The second problem is that those ingrained processes are transparent. ETS knows our processes better than we do. Remember, your children may spend hours a week thinking about the SAT, but the test-makers have spent decades thinking about their test and the students who take it. Again, ETS has studied your child's books, calculators, and curricula. High school teachers sit on College Board committees to discuss and develop content. All the while, the test-makers take notes.

I've been working lately with a student named Hannah, an enormously talented girl who, to all appearances, has always followed all the rules. She comes to tutoring on time, she always completes her homework, and she's unfailingly polite. Hannah, however, believes that she's not good at math. Consequently, she's underperforming on the math section of the SAT.

While I've taught Hannah how to do every math problem the test can throw at her, and while her SAT math skills have risen appreciably, her belief system about herself has remained stagnant. Every time she opens a math section of the SAT, her reflex reaction is, "Wow, these look tough." That was, after all, her reaction the first time she approached the test. Now, months later, having mastered each problem set individually, she still reverts to the ingrained belief that she can't figure out those tricky SAT math problems, all evidence to the contrary.

We'll talk about Hannah because her problem is such a common one, so typical of today's calculator-toting math students. With powerful calculators to do the heavy mental work, kids get used to making the grade in math class without actually becoming good at, or interested in, math. Especially in Washington, D.C., where we are located, surrounded by high-profile politicians, lobbyists, and attorneys, it can be tough for our high school students to get excited about math. These kids want to work on campaigns, become journalists, or head to law school—many of them just aren't interested in higher-level math. And enthusiasm and perceived skill level so often go hand in hand.

It's sometimes hard to believe that an outdated and disproved belief system about herself could really prevent Hannah from exercising skills she's already acquired. Taking a closer look at the questions the math section poses clarifies the situation. Let's take a look at a few sample problems to see why someone like Hannah might not recognize her own abilities.

EXPONENTS

Hannah is doing quite well in her upper-level math classes, thank you very much; she nailed exponents years ago. The SAT, however, frames things a bit differently. Hannah, like most high school students, is used to this kind of exponent:

$$x^2, y^3, z^4$$

She's comfortable performing complex operations such as:

$$\frac{4x^3y^2z}{2xyz} = 2x^2y$$

The SAT, however, switches things around a bit, occasionally throwing out problems such as:

$$4^x = 32^2$$

Hannah knows the rules of exponents and knows how to apply them, but somehow making the exponents variables instead of constants shakes her rule-oriented skill set, and she fumbles. She isn't even sure she knows how to punch this strange problem into her faithful calculator. The SAT made exponent problems familiar enough to Hannah that she felt she *should* know how to solve them, but different enough to seem impossible.

MADE UP MATH

The SAT positively delights in a fanciful creation often dubbed "Made Up Math." In this diabolical permutation of mathematics, the testmakers create a new, temporary math symbol and give it a definition. For instance, a typical made up math problem might look like this:

$$\text{Let } x\Omega y = (x - y)(x + y)$$
$$\text{What is } 3\Omega5 - 5\Omega3?$$

A careful and meticulous math student may well panic at the sight of a mathematical symbol he's never seen before. He may scan his memory, assume he's missed some crucial lecture back in algebra I, and conclude that this is a problem he is simply unequipped to answer.

As it turns out, ETS has here taken a simple concept—functions—and disguised it with unfamiliar symbology. All the student needed to do was translate the expression using the definition of the new symbol, Ω. The problem would then look like this:

$$(3-5)(3+5) - (5-3)(5+3)$$

And *that* is just simple arithmetic:

$$(-2)(8) - (2)(8)$$
$$-16 - 16$$
$$-32$$

While the made up math phenomenon was one Hannah could learn about and prepare for, the tactic ETS used here continued to plague her: present familiar-looking ideas in familiar packages and then give them an unexpected twist. Hannah could do the actual math, but getting the problems into a form that her calculator could handle was confusing. Without the confidence to keep plugging away, Hannah was lost.

REMAINDERS

Remember in third or fourth grade, when you were just learning long division, way before you knew about fractions or decimals? What did you do if the numbers didn't divide out evenly? You'd take whatever was left over and stick it next to your answer after a big R for remainder:

$$4\overline{)35} \atop \underline{32} \atop 3 $$ 8

8R3

Did you really remember that? Sure, now that you've been reminded, it's the simplest thing in the world. It's actually much easier than fractions or decimals, but only if you remember what it is. The SAT remembers, but expects its test-takers to have forgotten by the time they are in high school. Hannah did fine when I explained to her what they were asking, but on her own, she didn't have the presence of mind to figure that the test was asking for a concept she actually knew quite well. Again, the ideas were familiar ideas, changed just enough to discourage poor Hannah halfway through the problem. She had to learn how to be more creative.

BEHAVIORS THAT CRIPPLE CONFIDENCE

For the SAT math sections, presence of mind—thinking outside the box, being creative—can make all the difference. There will always be one or two devious new problems on the test that require creative thought as opposed to rote memorization. And that's where presence of mind is required. If a student's brain is occupied with filling in the correct bubbles, keeping track of the time, actively blocking out environmental distractions, and, most crucially, managing anxiety, there's often not a lot of energy left for truly creative thought.

For Hannah to be able to mentally step back from a problem far enough to access creativity, she needed to be calm. And to be calm, she needed to know that she could succeed on this test. She needed confidence. The math section, more than either of the other two sections on the SAT, absolutely requires absolute confidence. And that, after all of our work, was what Hannah was still missing.

Unfortunately, lack of stick-to-it-iveness isn't the only by-product of low confidence. Let's look at some of the other manifestations of low confidence on the math SAT. This list can serve as a sort of diagnostic chart; emergence of these symptoms often points to a diagnosis of low confidence. Take a look at the following behaviors.

Behavior 1: The Calculator Crutch

College Board allows students to bring in any one of a range of high-tech graphing calculators with, so I'm told, more computing capability than the first Apollo space shuttle. Students tend to be extremely dexterous on these little machines, having made full use of them in school. Students tend to heavily rely on these crutches.

The SAT is actually easier to do *without* a calculator, as long as you can do basic arithmetic. My students are shocked by this, and although I don't encourage anyone to go cold turkey, it's. With a calculator reassuringly in hand, students tend to overcomplicate and overcompute the simplest of problems. With such a powerful machine standing faithfully by, taking things the standard mathematics route becomes instinctive. Instead of pausing to ask what the easiest approach is, students reflexively punch buttons until their faithful machine provides a numerical solution.

Calculators also often increase computational errors, especially when a nervous teenager is punching the buttons. Additionally, because of the persuasive ethos of TI–83, the calculator of choice for my students, an impressive gadget can overrule a mere human's common-sense objections. I've had students tell me the area of a given square is negative 500 and then protest that the calculator stated that, so it must be true. I asked one incredulous student, "What is negative 14 squared?" knowing that it was beyond the times tables she had memorized. She dutifully plugged that into her calculator and announced, "Negative 196!" "OK," I allowed, "what about negative two squared?" She started to punch that into her calculator and then reconsidered, remembering that she already knew the answer. "Four!" she claimed. "Positive four?" I made sure. "Yes, positive four," she answered. "So, is a negative squared a positive?" was my final question. She paused, looked me in the eye, and answered, "Usually."

As proficient as these students are on their calculators, I've found many of them don't understand basic calculator syntax. While the TI–83 understands Order of Operations rules, it won't second-guess a student who punches buttons indiscriminately. Give a student the following problem, and you could get two very different answers:

$$4 + 8 \times 3 - 2$$

A student following established Order of Operations rules would compute the multiplication portion first, simplifying the problem to:

$$4 + 24 - 2$$

At this point, with all addition and subtraction left, he could perform the operations in any order and obtain the same result: 26. On his calculator, however, he might be tempted to punch in the problem just as it was originally given, hitting "enter" after each subcalculation. Even students who understand that it matters when you add and when you multiply often are so used to relying on their calculators for brainpower that they don't stop to think it out before hitting the keys. They might work through the problem this way:

$$4 + 8 = 12$$
$$12 \times 3 = 36$$
$$36 - 2 = 34$$

It all looks correct and official but, of course, the answer is wrong. On the SAT, ETS might helpfully supply "34" as an incorrect answer choice with just those students in mind.

Ultimately, a student who reflexively grabs a calculator usually does so because he's not immediately sure of the best way to go about doing the problem. Lack of confidence makes thinking it through not an option, so the student relies on the calculator to do the thinking. And when that student doesn't know which button solves that particular problem, he assumes that he is simply unable to solve that problem at all. There's no inherent problem with using a calculator. It just shouldn't be the only tool your child takes with him into the test. A student who figures out how to solve the problem and does so, and lets the calculator do the computations, is one who has overcome anxiety and lack of confidence, and who will be successful on the SAT.

Behavior 2: Too Many Formulas, Not Enough Thinking

Students tend to have trouble remembering the formula for determining the sum of the interior angles of a polygon. Unfortunately for them on the SAT, they tend to faithfully remember that there *is* a formula, and that they just don't remember what it is. A student who is focused on formula memorization often is trying to make up for a lack of confidence in her problem-solving abilities. Determining the sum of the interior angles of a polygon is really a matter of common sense, which is a lot harder to access during a stress-inducing test than a few stock formulas are.

Part of the problem of the timing of the SAT is that a good percentage of the students taking the test have moved far beyond algebra and geometry in their math studies at school. They not only may not remember some of the more basic formulas, the backbone set of math skills for the SAT, but they are unable to refrain from attempting to apply their higher math skills to the test. I've seen students flounder through a misguided application of trigonometry to a simple geometry problem on the SAT, while others get lost in a tangle of complicated equations when the answer was in actuality far simpler to reach.

Take the problem of the interior angles of a polygon. The SAT will give a student a misshapen hexagon, totally unfamiliar and sure to not match any of their textbook examples, and ask the student to find a certain interior angle. Rather than thinking: "I don't know a standard method for this, and the SAT doesn't test advanced methods, so there must be a common-sense way to determine that angle," students panic. They try to apply the Law of Sines. They attempt to determine the equations of the various line segments and have their calculators find the angles. They assume that because the SAT is asking for one angle, they have to be able to find them all. None of these methods will work, and the students assume that they are just not smart enough to do the math on the SAT. Actually, a polygon is just a collection of triangles, and if students can look at it that way, they'll very easily be able to determine the interior angles.

A student who worries too much about the substantive math skills required is often masking a sense of insecurity about his ability to think creatively and respond to new mathematical situations. A student who is constantly reaching for another formula is often just reaching for some artificial confidence. If your child is stressed about memorizing complex formulas for the SAT, he may need to change the way he thinks about the math SAT.

Behavior 3: Skipping Steps Is Cheating

Students believe that creativity is for art class. Math class requires discipline, structure, and rule-following. Right? Remember, for geometry teachers, it's "prove it my way" or "no credit." It's tricky telling students who have succeeded in math at school due to strictly following directions that they'll do better by chucking all of that out the window. A lot of students resist abandoning methods that have made them successful. It's not in their comfort zones.

One of the telltale signs that a student isn't being creative is right there in his test booklet. Neat rows of computations, step by step, indicate that this student is too focused on obeying the rules. That student can't let himself back-solve, guesstimate, or plug in numbers because it just doesn't seem right. He doesn't feel confident that he could find success any other way.

For some students, using tricks and strategies to get past some of the stickier math on the SAT feels like cheating. Some of them want to prove that they can do the test their way, the correct way, and still earn a sterling score. That's fine, although a bit unnecessarily self-punishing. Other students need to hang on to the methods they know because they're afraid of the uncharted waters. They lack the confidence to go it alone; they think they need the old methods to carry them along.

Behavior 4: Clean Practice Tests

Take a look at your son's last practice test, especially the math section. Did he scribble in calculations? Did he redraw diagrams to clarify the problem? Did he show any steps? Or could you reuse his test booklet for another student, because it's still pristine?

For a lot of students, having to write out steps on the math section is for wimps. They want to prove not just that they can do the math, but that they can do the math without the crutch of showing steps or writing down their calculations. Add that to the crutch of doing mainly calculator work, and you've got a clean test booklet at the end of a grueling test.

My students tell me that there's nothing wrong with not writing down every little thing, that they simply don't need to do that. While that can be true, the problem is that a student who is defiantly forbidding himself to write down *anything* is also most likely trying to prove that he's good enough to do the math. So not only do his scores generally suffer through the careless errors that jotting numbers down would catch, but he is highlighting a lack of confidence that may need to be addressed in other ways. Look at your child's test booklet—you may learn something.

Behavior 5: Faster Is Better

Remember taking timed multiplication table tests back in elementary school? Somewhere along the line, an alarming number of students have gotten in their heads that for math, faster is better. Set a timed test in front of them and that belief intensifies.

On the SAT, going too fast on the math section can be fatal. These questions often require four or five steps of calculations and a thorough rereading of the problem. A student racing the clock is unlikely to do that. Faster, on the SAT math section, is almost never better.

And, in a surprising twist, often students who work faster on the SAT math section do so less confidently. A student who is scared of running out of time and thus not snagging a top score will race through the math. A student who isn't terribly confident that her individual answers will be correct is motivated to try to answer a greater number of questions. And, if you think about it, it takes a great deal of confidence to take your time and work carefully while the clock is ticking.

Pay attention when your child takes a practice test—how concerned about timing is she? When those math scores come back, you may see calculation errors, unfinished problems, misunderstood questions, wrong answers that are the result of not reading carefully, or even answers bubbled into the wrong circles. You may be looking at a confidence problem that needs to be addressed.

***

As should be clear from these examples, all of these reactions (or over-reactions) are indications of anxiety and confidence issues. Under pressure, people stay within their comfort zones. They adhere to, or even revert to, the processes that are most deeply ingrained in them. We want to expand students' comfort zones, to give them a bigger array of methods to use and make sure that they feel adept with these new processes. Then, we can help them by constantly encouraging them to use the method that is best for them, regardless of whether their 7th grade math teacher would approve.

Taking the SAT can feel as stressful to your child as living through a Wild West gunfight, with bullets flying all around her. In such life or death situations, most people are tempted to let loose with whatever weaponry they have available to them, as fast as they possibly can. I can take the SAT faster than most human beings because I have more skills and experience with the SAT than the typical test-taker. More importantly, however, I take the SAT faster because I pause at the beginning of every question to consider the best way to go about answering that question. Pausing to look for the easiest way to answer a math question is a lot like not being the quickest draw with a gun but having the surest shot. Having that surety is ultimately faster, more invigorating, and more confidence-building.

Underconfidence, as always, requires a multipronged approach. For Hannah, we eventually reached a point at which the accumulated stack of successful practice tests convinced her that she was something of a math superstar, and no mere SAT was going to throw her. She needed to see the success in scaled scores before she could believe it.

Most of my students who have slogged through life convinced that they are irrevocably doomed as math students lean more toward another approach. They tend to respond more eagerly to the idea that the math section of the SAT is not about math. As they see that even math geeks get thrown, and that the survival skills they've adopted in countless math classes will be rewarded here, they start to see the math section as a challenge they are ready for.

Ultimately, success does not come until a student rejects the notion that being "bad at math" is determined in 7th grade. Parents, teachers, coaches, and siblings can all assist in helping a suffering student see all the challenges in life she's already conquered. Math is just one more challenge, and the fight isn't over yet.

We'll talk more in this book about confidence—about how to help your child feel more confident and build a culture of confidence in your family. It's an endeavor worth attempting, and not just for the SAT scores. In my experience, confidence is the very best thing students can take with them on the day of the test—and not just for that math score.

CHAPTER FOUR

Wrestling with the Writing Section

Many of the students who walk into my office to talk about the new SAT have one thing on their minds: the essay. One by one they report the rumors they've assumed are true: the essay counts for a whopping one-third of your entire SAT score; you have to use one example from Shakespeare and one from American history; if you spell even one word wrong you're doomed; if you include a personal experience that's not quite true, ETS will track down the truth and give you a zero. There's one rumor none of them seem to have heard: many colleges, lacking a past history with this new admissions device, are largely ignoring it.[1]

While the essay is claiming more than its fair share of collective anxiety, the other part of the SAT writing section, the multiple-choice grammar portion, tends not to merit the anxious attentions of the teenage rumor mill much at all. The adult world of parents, educators, and college admissions officers is paying attention nonetheless, and expressing just as much concern for the grammar as for the essay itself. You can't blame us for worrying, especially when you realize just what's being tested in those two multiple-choice grammar sections. You'll worry even more when you realize just how large a percentage of the total SAT score those few grammar questions claim.

It's not as if ETS created the current writing section out of thin air. The multiple-choice grammar section existed in the Test of Standard Written English (TSWE) way back when. It was yanked off the revised SAT in 1994, but reemerged on the PSAT a year later. All along it was enthroned as the SAT II Writing test that high school students have been taking for the past several years. Finally, these multiple-choice questions have come full circle, reentering the SAT I as the writing section of the test.[2] Phew!—it's been a long journey for a set of somewhat arbitrary and bizarre grammar questions. Understandably, colleges aren't too sure what to make of this new SAT score portion. That's good news for your child, because most high school students aren't too sure what to make of this section of the test, either.

GRAMMAR AND USAGE

The grammar portion of the writing section of the new SAT pinpoints the deviation between formal standard written English and the way that we actually speak the language. In other words, the little, technically incorrect expressions and speech habits we read in newspapers, hear from our teachers and on TV are the subject of the grammar test. If this seems a little unfair, consider this: Most high schools in America have dramatically cut down or eliminated English grammar from their curriculums over the past generation. We're testing our kids on writing the language in a way that they often don't hear and haven't learned in school. It makes you wonder why the grammar portion is on the SAT at all.

My favorite example is singular versus plural possessive pronouns— and for those of you who had their last grammar lesson back in elementary school, I'll give you an example. Even many educated people will say "everyone has their own car." You may even catch that usage somewhere in this book. Old school grammarians would of course tell us that it's "everyone has his own car," but in current language usage this seems sexist—a big no-no in progressive writing classes and mixed company of all sorts. You could say "everyone has her own car," which would be grammatically correct and feel fine, so long as we knew that only women or girls were being talked about. Finally, one could be uber-proper and say "everyone has his or her own car." But this gets a bit unwieldy if the sentence continues with "everyone has his or her own car and he or she must be sure to park his or her own car in his or her designated parking space or he or she will get a ticket." Good grief! "Everyone has their own car" it is, except on the SAT.

Another sticky area of grammar testing is termed "prepositional idiom." As I explain to my students, certain words like certain prepositions or conjunctions. We might think of this phenomenon as conversational habit; ETS claims it to be grammatical necessity. Some of these are easy: you depend *on* someone, you contribute *to* something. Others are more subtle: "different *from*" is used differently from "different *than*." Still other groupings must be memorized painstakingly before the SAT: if you use "not only," it must be followed later in the sentence with "but also." When students get deep enough into the grammar subtleties they must learn by rote for the SAT, it can be hard to get them to believe that this test is anything other than arbitrary.

By far the trickiest area of grammar testing on the SAT is word choice. Some of the sentences that students must check for errors contain a word that isn't right for the meaning of the sentence. These are easily confused word pairs, such as *indifferent* for *not different*, or *discrete* for *discreet*. The problem with testing word choice is simply that to the students it looks like a spelling test, and they're not thinking about spelling. For students assiduously ferreting out grammatical errors, a minor spelling error won't get noticed—they're just not looking for it. On a spelling test they'll do just fine. On a grammar test, they'll find the grammatical errors. Mix them up and don't tell them there might be misused words, and they'll miss those questions every time. My favorite question begins "The principle doctrines of physics include . . ." Students who know that *principle* should be *principal* will still gloss over that *principle* tucked in snugly next to a word (doctrines) that means "principles." That question alone should turn ETS-believers into cynics. After all, even ETS gets the grammar wrong sometimes.[3] This test isn't trying to make sure high school students develop great writing skills; this test is trying to persuade smart, prepared students into filling out the contours of a bell curve.

So what should a careful student do to conquer this test? My experience is that the majority of people can get the majority of the grammar questions correct simply by using their ears. Reading questions "out loud" is a great help. Obviously, you can't give an oral recitation of the questions during the test, but the act of mumbling, or subaudiblization as the linguists would say, effectively tricks the brain into thinking it has heard things as though they had been said out loud. People tend to get much of the test right because they've adopted the patterns of the intelligent and educated people around them, such as their parents and teachers. Unfortunately, they get the remainder of the test wrong because they've adopted the incorrect speech patterns from these same people. For students who approach English as a second language, however, that ingrained "sense" of what sounds right and what sounds wrong may be quite a bit harder to develop.

The solution is easy enough—students simply need to be made aware of the specific points of grammar that are tested on the SAT. They have to then practice reviewing previous errors so that they learn and understand the rules of grammar and can push aside the patterns heard in daily life. I encourage students to actively review previous questions immediately before taking a test in order to put themselves into the grammar mode.

The worst part, then, for an anxious student, is remaining calm enough to "speak" the sentence in her head, and then confident enough to circle a word or phrase that sounds wrong to her. On the sentence improvement section, a student must choose one of five permutations of a sentence based not just on grammatical correctness, but also on clarity. There's just a lot of self-trust required to read the sentence five times in five different ways and select the option that sounds least garbled. Especially when a student does not have any actual idea what the grammatical rule is that supports his choice, it is difficult to be confident enough to quickly circle that answer and move on to the next question. Naturally, the next question will also include an incorrect permutation of the structured grammar that a student may only know on an intuitive level.

That's a lot of self-confidence required for a kid who may not have received a sterling grade on his last English essay. When just one question eludes him, it's tough to stay calm and loose enough to give the next one a fair shot. For this portion of the test, however, the list of rules tested is limited enough that straight practice works to convince the humblest students that they have skills enough to trust their gut. When their gut can't help them out, running through that list provides an easy and comforting process to keep them working and confident. Again, however, all the knowledge in the world can't help a student who is too tense or unsure to access his intuitive knowledge of English.

THE ESSAY

Would you want to write for 25 minutes on one of the following topics?

Power corrupts even the best of men. Do you agree or disagree?
All change requires sacrifice. Do you agree or disagree?
The more things change, the more they remain the same. Do you agree or disagree?
Freedom of speech is the most important right we have. Do you agree or disagree?

Remember, you have to support your ideas with examples from history, literature, current events, or personal experience. Use a number 2 pencil and don't forget that the clock is ticking.

Chances are, no matter how educated or brilliant you are, your mind is now racing to think of good people who let power corrupt them. Julius Caesar? Or who was the guy who ended up killing him? Once again, ETS has caught us. Instead of calmly reasoning out how we may feel about a particular prompt question, we're frantically trying to come up with the most impressive example of power corrupting good men. We've haven't even considered taking the opposite side, have we? And we certainly don't have any solid reasoning to back up our position. Once again, ETS knows how we think and is taking advantage of that.

If most of us fell for it (and I'm not saying all of you did), think about those innocent 16-year-olds walking into that test with half-formed impressions of the world based on the five works of literature they've managed to plow through so far in their high school English curriculum. What are the odds that during the SAT, they're feeling calm enough to remember who killed Caesar, much less calm enough to write naturally and freely on such artificial and constrained topics?

The most important thing for teens to remember about the essay portion of the SAT is to stay calm and be themselves. Really. The essay scorers have read hundreds of sterile essays on *Huckleberry Finn*, and they'd be thrilled to get an honest, heartfelt look at your daughter's summer camp experience sinking her canoe. They already know who killed Julius Caesar and want instead to hear your son's reasoning when he claims that freedom of religion is more important than freedom of speech.

A student who is overly anxious will panic on first reading the essay prompt. An instant "I know nothing about this!" reaction is inevitable, and the next step typically will be furiously thrashing about for meaningful and impressive-sounding examples to use to support a topic the student believes he knows nothing about. The resulting essay will be shallow at best, not having sprung from reasoned and rational analysis.

A calm and confident student, on the other hand, has an idea that he can do this and knows how. He reads the essay prompt and allows himself time for reflection before deciding how he'll go about answering the question. After his approach is determined, he then selects examples that support the position he has chosen. His reasoning forms the backbone of the essay; the examples add depth and authority to his argument.

If that sounds a bit too good to be true, you're concentrating too much on the 25-minute time constraint. As with the rest of the SAT, but even more so on the essay, perceptions of time limitations are far more damaging than the time limitations themselves. As it turns out, panicking and rushing through it really doesn't help a student's score—he may be able to write more on the essay or include a few more generic examples, but the quality and style of his work will take a nose dive.

In fact, the readers and scorers of the essay are instructed not to grade specifically on length and not to deduct for an unfinished essay. Writing as much as possible of a good essay is therefore better than writing the entirety of a mediocre one. Again, however, remaining calm and confident is required. Otherwise, how could a student really stop herself from jumping into writing before she's considered her topic sufficiently?

As miraculous as it may seem, when students stop and think about what they're going to write, and stay true to their personalities in the writing, their essays will not only be better, they will probably be longer too. They'll get so involved in the writing of something that they are passionate about that they won't worry about how to fill up two short pages. Of course, all of that requires the confidence to not let anxiety get the better of you.

This is also contrary to rumor. Michael Winerip wrote a *New York Times* article titled "SAT Essay Test Rewards Length and Ignores Errors of Fact."[4] Interestingly, he declared upon analysis of all the ETS-released essay samples that the longer the essay, the better the score. Just write as much as you can and you're golden. ETS disagrees, not surprisingly. The ETS people stick by their earlier pronouncement that the scorers don't discriminate based on length, and that a really well-written short essay will always win a higher score than a poorly written lengthy tome.

So is longer better? The Winerip study seems to prove it, but we'd say that's a correlation, not a causality. The high-scoring essays were longer because they were better. In a short period of time under pressure, it's relatively easy to write a large amount about something that you're very knowledgeable about and care about, and quite difficult to write something that you don't know much about and couldn't care less about.

Bad writing, especially on these essays, is the equivalent of stammering. People are treading water and trying to think of what to say next, but not really making any progress. They end up with half an essay about a half-formed idea that uses half the space given to them. Additionally, students who are insecure about their writing and unsure of their position on the topic often try to insert impressive vocabulary words, which can end up sounding artificial, awkward, or just plain wrong. When people write about something they're knowledgeable about, they write in a way that's confident, that flows, that has a lot to say, and that uses all the space allocated. The impressive words aren't necessary; the essay itself will be impressive. The higher score and the greater length are both attributed to writing about something that you know.

> *Nathaniel was not, in any sense, a strong reader. His preliminary SAT scores told that story eloquently: Math 730, Verbal 420. He attended a high school where, my sense was, he never really had to read anything that was assigned to him and could get by with CliffsNotes, paying attention in class, and a little bit of effort.*
>
> *He wrote an essay for the SAT that was, to be frank, atrocious. The prompt was something like, "Are people basically good or basically bad?" and his essay purportedly used Ralph Waldo Emerson to answer that question. It went something like this: "People aren't basically good but actually are basically bad. For example, Emersen [sic] thought people were bad so he went to live in the woods. If people weren't bad, maybe he would have stayed home where he could've watched TV or gone out to the movies once in a while so he wouldn't have to write so much."*

I asked him about the essay he wrote, and he replied, "Yeah, well, I didn't really know much about the topic." But he, for some reason, felt he had to use a literary example, even if he knew nothing about it. He wrote about Emerson as only one who has never read Emerson could.

So I asked him what he was an expert on. He thought for a minute and volunteered, "Sports!" "OK," I said, "sports are good, but what else?" He thought and he thought and came up with, "Basketball!" Sports it was.

Nathaniel wrote a lot of practice essays for me. Any topic I gave him that had to do with success, he wrote about Michael Jordan and the Chicago Bulls. Any topic I gave him that had to do with failure, he wrote about the Washington Bullets. His essays were not prewritten or mechanical, but he became very adept at writing about sports to answer the questions in the essay prompts.

Nathaniel's essay for the actual SAT was something to the effect of "Describe an event that changed history." His answer? "When Michael Jordan entered the NBA draft in 1984, it was an event that changed history. Jordan not only surpassed all notions of what it meant to be a professional basketball player, but also changed the role of professional athletes in American society." And it went on confidently from there. Ten out of twelve. For Nathaniel, a miracle.

Write about what you know. It really works.

Have your children practice essays on ideas that they would hope to use the day of the test. They won't walk in with prewritten essays so much as a few really good examples that can be tailored to fit the topics given to them. This will keep your teen from blanking out at first glimpse of that essay topic. The essay prompts are designed so that many different types of examples can be used, so that students aren't doomed if they lack expertise on some narrow field of learning. Whatever the topic, they can use their interests and passions to answer the question.

For example, an essay topic from years ago asked essentially "Do critics perform a necessary role in society?" Without a set of examples to draw from, most people made the mistake of writing about the obvious critics they knew: movie critics and restaurant critics. For most of them, those, again, ended up being half-baked examples that made a half-formed essay and, at best, a halfway decent score. My student had walked in feeling confident about using Dr. Martin Luther King Jr. and the Civil Rights Movement as her example that she would try to work into the essay, no matter what the question. She was able to use her pet example very effectively to answer this topic. "As a critic of race relations in 1950s America, Martin Luther King Jr. effectively changed American society for the better." And so on.

Go one step further: Become an expert on the things you would like to write on. Initially this same student had written an essay about Dr. King—she knew all the broad themes of what had made him an effective leader but was short on detail; her essays got about two-thirds of the way through and then petered out. How did he effectively help end segregation? Um, by giving a lot of speeches, and organizing protests. Good—and what did that do? Um, make people realize that segregation was wrong. OK, so how did that end segregation? Uh, did I mention his speeches? By rereading the *Encyclopedia Britannica* entry on Dr. King, this student was able to fill subsequent essays with an extra handful of facts, making her writing more confident, more effective, and ultimately longer. Knowing that King's "I Have a Dream" speech in 1963 prompted the political ground swell that led to the landmark Civil Rights Act of 1964 and Voting Rights Acts of 1965 helped. Less stammering. For another student, just taking the time to look up Schindler's first name and how it was spelled (Oskar) helped her write an essay that was more solid in detail. More importantly, it helped her feel more prepared to attack whatever topic ETS assigned her.

Ultimately, the essay portion of the SAT plays the same trick on students that the rest of the SAT does. It makes students feel inadequate and unprepared by surprising them with topics or ideas they aren't expecting. A student who understands the test and the testmakers is able to step back from the initial panic and realize that there's never anything unfamiliar about the SAT. A prepared student always has enough information to answer any question on the SAT. I remind my students of this over and over again: you know all the math formulas you need, there's enough information in the passage to answer the question, and you can use *For Whom the Bell Tolls* or the Civil War to respond to any essay prompt they throw at you. When your son realizes that what he has is good enough for the SAT, he'll be able to stop panicking and start getting creative.

BE ORGANIZED, BE DETAILED

Imagine that the people reading and scoring these essays are underemployed, disgruntled, bleary-eyed recent English grads and teachers who are reading their fifty-sixth essay for the day and are really unhappy about that. You won't be far from the truth. Students need to make it easy for them with a straightforward, easy-to-follow structure and a lot of detail to support the thesis. The task is not to write a great piece of literature, but to answer a question with a solid piece of reasoning and a cogent example. One client described it to me as the courtroom attorney model: tell them what you're going to say, tell them, and then tell them what you told them. Accomplishing this will get a solid score.

Superior scores generally will require more complex thought, diversity of sentence structure, and higher level diction. People who are naturally very good writers will employ those tactics naturally. People who have trouble with writing will often worry about those same things, but not have the basics of structure and supportive detail and miss out on getting a solid score.

What you don't want is to let underconfidence or anxiety keep your child from doing a basically good job on a basic essay. Anyone can write clearly, as long as that's really what they're trying to do. Anxiety can trick students into transforming their own standard writing style into a torturous attempt to impress that can only result in a falsely pretentious essay with no discoverable foundation or structure. Stay basic, and stay calm.

When it comes to the SAT, staying calm is always the best way to success. For teens, they don't need to be told again that they can't do this, they can't achieve that score, they can't write a strong essay. They need to be shown how to use the skills they already have to achieve what they thought they couldn't. After all, that's the core of confidence—not that you've been shown some trick or method that will save the day, but that you've been shown that all along you've had the skills to save the day on your own.

Just as Nathaniel found a way to use his superior sports knowledge to conquer the essay portion of the test, so other students can discover the skills they've developed that they thought were useless. The SAT, in the view of most of the world, promotes and rewards a certain narrow type of intelligence. If you've got it, you win. If you don't, too bad. No wonder teenagers are stressed out.

The great news is that it's simply not true. If you show a guy who's admittedly *not* a word guy, *not* a reader, *not* a writer a way he *can* do this test his way, assuring him that the things he can do are terrific, then he'll walk in to take that test with self-confidence. He'll walk in saying to himself that he can give them exactly what they want. A kid who walks into the SAT with that much self-confidence is sure to do his best, no matter what they throw at him.

After all the rumors, all the controversy, and all the hype, the writing section of the new SAT is by far the easiest section of the test, not to mention the section that colleges pay the least amount of attention to. If your child knows what is on the test, practices, and has a plan for the essay, your child should feel confident on the writing section. And that confidence is just what teens need to succeed.

III

Underperformance

The Manifestations

CHAPTER FIVE

Anxiety

Sally's parents had her begin to prep for the SAT in her sophomore year. "She's a terrible test-taker," her father related pragmatically, and Sally, sitting on the couch next to him, nodded her agreement. An A– student at one of the best private schools in the area, Sally nevertheless knew she needed a 2100 on the SAT to have a shot at attending her dream school: Dad's alma mater, Williams College.

Preparation began in the usual way, reviewing the relevant content, brushing up rusty math topics. Insights to the test and test-taking strategies complemented the conventional methods she had learned in school—plugging numbers into math problems with variables in order to circumvent ponderous algebra, for instance. It was all standard test prep stuff. Diagnostic tests indicated that time was only a slight problem. Her scores were strong and progressively getting stronger.

A couple of weeks before the test, she was firmly in command of the needed skills and it looked like she would clobber the test. "I doubt it," she replied almost jauntily, "I always panic on these types of tests. My dad says it runs in the family—he did really poorly on his SAT too."

All evidence to the contrary, Sally already had her outcome clearly in mind. Two weeks before the test date, she hadn't even begun to chip away at her most formidable obstacle: herself. Despite weeks of effort, she believed she hadn't changed at all, and sure

enough, she was right. On her first practice test, Sally panicked,
rushing through the test and missing nearly half of the questions.

The fact is that everyone who takes the SAT—from insecure adolescents feeling that their futures are riding on the test to seasoned tutors—experiences some form of anxiety. What complicates this is that anxiety interacts with a number of other factors to produce underperformance. Because anxiety is a product of the interaction between expectation and knowledge, or lack of knowledge, it's useful to pick apart the pieces of test performance and deal with them individually before putting them together to see how the interaction affects testing.

There are, of course, differences in intelligence, knowledge, and work ethic. Some people exert the minimum and still seem to be high achievers. Others may be less "naturally gifted," and simply work harder to achieve the same high scores. As my grandfather would tell me, "Make up with your feet what God didn't put in your head." The SAT, however, can't tell the difference. As I tell my students, a really lucky guesser will get the exact same score as a true math geek.

Phenomenal luck aside, no one will secure a perfect score, no matter how bright, without a certain body of core knowledge. An infinite body of knowledge without some ability to apply it intelligently will likewise come to naught. We all have a blend of raw intelligence and knowledge coupled with our attitudes that dictate how successful we'll be. And the attitudes tend to cause the most problems.

While we can measure knowledge and test our intelligence within a confined arena, attitude remains an area over which we have less control. I knew Sally was intelligent; I made sure she had all the knowledge she needed to ace the SAT. She needed to change her attitude about herself and the test before she could begin to attack her anxiety. When it came down to it on test day, her attitude would determine her anxiety level and thus her score.

Sally and I redesigned her plan of study, getting her on a steady program of affirmation of her abilities, disavowals that the SAT says much about her, and, to desensitize her to testing conditions, a practice regimen of actual SATs with scores she planned in advance to cancel.[1] Slowly, as she built up an arsenal of strong scores and a real sense of personal accomplishment, Sally began to change the way she felt about herself, and then to change the way she felt about the SAT. And, finally, when she had conquered her own anxiety surrounding the test, she was able to conquer the SAT.

Ultimately, the limits that people place on themselves have far more impact than any external limits. This simply means that belief systems matter. Good coaches, whether for the SAT or for golf, recognize this truth and help their charges to get out of their own way. Sally was limited by her own perception of her ability to stay cool under the pressure of testing. If my student believes she will succeed, she is probably right. If she believes she will fail, she is almost certainly right. And when Sally told me she'd panic on the real test, I didn't bet against her. To paraphrase Richard Bach, argue for your limitations and they are yours.[2]

Later in this chapter, we'll discuss why Sally's attitude was so defeatist—you may have already picked up on some of the clues—and how she came to believe the way she did. We'll also discuss the particular route her anxiety took—panic, one of several common manifestations of anxiety. More importantly, we'll talk about how Sally and many other students overcame both their attitudes and underperformance difficulties.

DIAGNOSING ANXIETY

Diagnosis and treatment of anxiety overlap substantially. This means that just figuring out what's going on empowers many kids enough to let them control it. For some, finding and treating the cause allows them to overcome the symptoms, while for others, learning to overcome the symptoms helps them conquer whatever is causing the anxiety.

Let me suggest the following list as a place to begin thinking about the kinds of issues and problems that could be affecting your teen's testing ability. These questions and ideas work for both parents and students, so share it with your child. Use it as a starting point to discover what the problems may be and where the solutions may lie.

1.   Learn about the test. Find out how it is structured, how it is scored, and how it is used in admissions decisions. Knowledge leads to a feeling of better control, which leads to lowered anxiety. The less mystery the SAT holds, the more capable your teen will feel going in to take the test.

2. Ask yourself honestly what the SAT means to you. A chance to prove something? A measure of self-worth? An indication of intelligence? A shot at a dream school? Then ask yourself what a "good" score is and decide what numbers would make you happy. If you don't have a goal, you'll never be able to tell if you succeeded.

3. Determine where the negative stress is coming from. This is a process, involving observing family members, different stressful situations, and some introspection. If you can't find the stress source, chances are you can't fight it.

4. Think long term. The SAT score itself gets you nothing: what is it that you want to gain by this test? Be realistic about not just colleges, but majors, careers, and financial aid—everything that goes along with college.

5. Ask yourself whether feeling concerned about test performance needs to be such a bad thing. Not all stress is bad, and not all symptoms of stress are destructive. Believe it or not, students can learn to use the adrenaline and intensity of anxiety to increase energy and focus on the test. Let's turn old-fashioned, sweaty-palmed stress into high-adrenaline, high-scoring SATs!

6. Study smart. Just doing massive amounts of practice testing will only make the stress worse without teaching better performance. We'll talk about ways to make studying not only more efficient, but more likely to result in a calm, stress-free test day.

Let's start by talking about how to identify the problem. If we can find out exactly what is happening when Sally puts her pencil to the answer sheet, we're in a better position to fix the situation. Most of us are imperfect diagnosticians of our own problems as well as the problems of others. This only intensifies when we try to diagnose our own children through the lens of our own experience, illusions (or delusions), and expectations. We cast their lives in the light of our own lives and project our testing angst onto them. Maybe Sally's father was feeling his own test anxiety when he told me she was a terrible test-taker.

When people underperform, in any realm, it can be difficult to know why that underperformance occurred. We've all heard the excuses—"he's just not any good at this type of thing," "she chokes under pressure," "you just didn't study enough," "I was really tired that day," "it was just a bad day." Was it knowledge, intelligence, attitude, or an amalgam of factors?

Attributing underperformance to the wrong cause can worsen an already bad situation. At the very least, it will misdirect time and effort from the real culprit. At the worst, it can reduce a bright kid with a minor performance glitch to a self-saboteur with much more serious problems than the SAT.

Teasing out the causative factors of underperformance is difficult and messy work. Unlike laboratory experiments with strict controls and clearly defined variables, teenagers, particularly, are constantly in flux. Their schedules are rarely routine. They are still forming and reforming their habits. Throw extracurricular academic pressures into the mix, and things go from unpredictable to downright wacky.

My Golf Swing Isn't Yours

Diagnosing someone else's anxiety problem is as difficult as fixing someone else's golf swing. I might, with the best of intentions, suggest to my golf buddy that he could fix his swing by not overswinging the club. That is, after all, what worked for me, so it would be a natural fix to suggest. But what if that's not his problem? Now he's focusing on his swing when the real issue is his stance. He hasn't tackled the fundamentals, hasn't improved his swing, has no plan or remedy and is seeing no results. In addition to his golf problem, he now adds greater frustration and self-doubt as his best corrective efforts are failing, and growing resentment toward me as I keep harping on him not to overswing with the misbegotten idea that I am actually helping. He becomes irritated with me, and I with him, as I defensively insist that I am only trying to help. Golf is now a lot less fun and we sure aren't getting better scores.

Now play out that scene as I've frequently seen it played in my office. A well-meaning father, frantic to ensure that his daughter snags the desired college acceptance, insists that she study the way he studied for the California bar exam 30 years ago. A concerned mother feels that her son is just not putting in the study time she's heard he needs to really nail the math section. In an academic setting, where the results arguably matter, the outcome is the same as on the golf course: The SAT is a lot less fun and we sure aren't getting better scores.

Instead of issues of ego about athletic prowess in golf, we are tapping into insecurities about intelligence and academic ability that are close to the core of self-identity. Amplify it within a family, and we're dealing with living up to a father's crackerjack legal career or a mother's pristine graduate school transcript. We've pulled in parental concerns for their children's success and happiness and their own needs for validation of being good parents. More crucially for test performance, we've made the test about dad's or mom's expectations, not the teen's potential.

As you can imagine, or as you have already experienced, things can get really unhappy, really fast. Now instead of a minor testing problem, we have major test anxiety, family tension, and a deterioration of the parent-child relationship just when that child needs more support than ever. The harder the parent pushes, the worse the problem gets.

So, what's the solution? Let me suggest a few commonalties among the families I've worked with over the past 15 years. These are typical trouble spots, blockages to diagnosis and communication, as well as suggestions to foster communication and healthier testing. These may not fit your family, but the odds are pretty good that at least some of them do. One of these issues may be the very thing that is troubling your son or daughter, or, the very thing that is keeping *you* from understanding what is troubling your teen.

Remember that test-taking and teenagers are two very complex entities. Chances are that what was happening when Sally started testing was a combination of many forces in her life, from her past experiences to her parents' expectations to her own fear of failure. Just because it's complicated doesn't mean it's impossible to solve, as any good SAT-taker knows.

WHAT PARENTS CAN DO TO PREVENT ANXIETY

Let Go of Your Own Testing Anxieties

Part of understanding how a student feels about the SAT is finding out how that student's parents feel about the SAT. Maybe it's not surprising that the factor that tends to influence a teenager's perception of the test the most is his parents' perceptions of the test. In turn, those perceptions of the SAT are still heavily influenced by the personal experiences those parents have had with testing in high school and in college. I'm pretty sure that if parents had to tell the truth, quite a few of them would still remember their educational "vital statistics"—GPA, major test scores, class rank, for instance. I also have a feeling, that for some of those parents, those numbers still play into their self-images in some small way.

In other words, it's often not just the student's insecurities that are being played out on test day, but the parents', whether they be personal (such as old test scores) or familial (wanting their kids to get into better schools than their sisters' kids did). Too many students start to suspect that when Dad's yelling at them to practice SAT vocabulary, he's not always merely concerned with their own future happiness and well-being. They start to suspect that Dad's nervousness and anxiety mean that there's a good chance they'll really blow it on the SAT. And that can really make a kid nervous.

It makes you stop and think. A child's SAT score says a lot about her parents—just not in the way we usually assume. A good score doesn't make a good parent any more than a bad score makes a bad parent, but underperformance might just be an indication that those parents have inadvertently projected their own outgrown anxieties onto their child to her detriment.

That sounds a bit harsh, doesn't it? It's natural, though, for a child to sense the importance his parents are putting on any test, and this test is, in fact, important. The particularly pernicious part of this phenomenon is when a parent's insecurities add pressure on a student to perform for more than just himself. This sends the message that the SATs do, after all, decide who is smart and who is dumb, and that message is both incorrect and destructive to a test-taker.

The second danger area is in comparison of a parent's scores and college acceptances with a child's. Let me explain why this intergenerational transmutation of SAT stress is so dangerous. Students today face a very different college application landscape than other generations. Just ten years ago, elite educational institutions accepted a much higher percentage of applicants, and a pretty good SAT score could guarantee a slot in any number of great schools. This decade's students are competing against many times more applicants for what feels like an ever-shrinking number of slots.[3]

The sometimes subtle, sometimes silent pressure to live up to parents or siblings may present students with an impossibility in today's academic environment. For families in which achievement is an important part of their culture, success often is defined by mom or dad's alma mater, which, since their matriculations decades ago, has certainly upped its entrance requirements. The subtle or not-so-subtle pressure to be a university legacy student can cause crippling anxiety on test day.

In short, be aware of how you talk about this test. Don't let it assume an inappropriate importance in your household. When you talk about the test, ask questions, don't lecture. Find out how your child feels about the test and let that be the foundation for discussion.

VALIDATE, LISTEN, VALIDATE

Over the years I have tutored thousands of high school students from all backgrounds and family structures, and the one thing that almost all of these teenagers seemed in desperate need of was sincere adult validation. It seems there is no such thing as too much positive affirmation.

Unfortunately, some teenagers tend to discount anything positive their parents say and amplify anything negative. It can be helpful to assume that nearly every word you say to your teen may be perceived as criticism. That sounds extreme, but it's a useful place to start evaluating your discourse. Listen carefully during your next conversation with your teenager. If he is saying "Yeah, I know," he's feeling criticized. The natural impulse is to repeat your point, to emphasize its importance, and your teenager then stops listening. Soon, anything you say on that topic will be subsumed under this dynamic of criticism, and the cycle becomes nearly unbreakable.

Try a different approach. Always precede instruction, advice, and especially criticism with a validation first. Take a look at Table 5.1 to see how parent-teenager communication often breaks down. It's just more likely that your teen will get the message if it's framed in a way he can hear and accept.

Parents tell me that this is easy advice to give when the outcome really isn't important. For the SAT, many ask me to try to strike fear

Table 5.1

You Said	You Meant	Your Child Heard
You can't expect to do well on the test if you don't get a good night's sleep.	Go to bed early, so you'll have a chance of doing well on the test.	You're not responsible enough to make even basic decisions, and you're not going to do well on the test.
I'm really impressed with how hard you are working, and I wonder if going to bed a bit earlier might also help you to do well.	Go to bed early, so you'll have a chance of doing well on the test.	You're doing a great job in preparing for the test, and might want to also go to bed early to make sure you'll do well.
We want you to do well on this test, but we love you no matter what your score is.	This is an important test and it's important to us that you do your best.	This test is really important, and we're worried because we think you're going to blow it.
We really love you and are proud of how hard you've worked to do well on this test.	We want you to do well on this test, and we think encouraging you is the best way to be supportive.	You're a capable, responsible person, and we're sure you'll do well.

into their child's heart or threaten their child with views of the bleak existence awaiting those who are only average performers. Fear is not a really great motivator, at least not over any period of time. In the short-term, sure. But to get the best of a student, motivation needs to come from within. Encourage your child. Don't frighten him. You cannot keep frightening a child to prod him to work, lest you bring about one of these outcomes:

1. Risk blowing your credibility by crying wolf
2. Induce anxiety in your child that will in fact hurt his performance
3. Do harm to your child's self-confidence and relationship with you, things that are much more important than the SAT.

The fact is, stress can be a major problem on the SAT. Stress can rob teens of focus and energy just when they need it most. Students who feel stressed can have trouble with memory and processing. Scaring your child really can make him do *worse* on the test instead of better.

It's when the outcome is important that kids need to know they're trusted. I've had students whose parents completely took over the college admissions process, only allowing them to see the applications when a signature was needed. I've been micromanaged in tutoring by overly anxious parents while the teen rolled her eyes and mentally disengaged from the test preparation process. The message these kids get is that they're not capable of coming through when it counts. As important as the SAT might be, this is utterly contrary to what we need to teach our children for their long-term success in life. And it's not going to help them on the day of the SAT either.

Imagine two kids with identical knowledge bases and identical intelligence levels. The student who has heard only positive things from her parents about herself and her ability to master this test will have a dramatic advantage over the student who actually expends energy during the test worrying about what her parents are going to think of her. There's no need to scare these kids—they're already scared. What these kids need to know is that they are capable of doing well.

Pay Attention to Neighborhood Buzz

Keep your ears open. What is being said around you about the SAT? What is the school guidance counselor saying? What about the other kids at school and their parents? Listen carefully to the voices that your child may be listening to and may be believing. Not all of these voices are accurate, and the odds are good that most of them aren't calming.

Talk with your child's teachers to get a sense of test behavior and concerns in the classroom. Talk with your child's friends—they'll be more willing to share how their group is dealing with testing pressures. Of course, talk with your child, asking questions and listening carefully to the responses for hints of what may really be affecting your child on test day.

Inform with Facts

Lastly, parents should share what they know about this test—that it is one hurdle in a series of hurdles. The students should know that the test is predictable and that it doesn't measure intelligence. They should also be thoroughly acquainted with the grading and scoring system of the SAT. Knowledge is power. Facts create comfort and comfort creates confidence. For the students, education has become increasingly relative: they learn competing theories of history, they argue sides in political debates, they learn about disagreements even in the field of science. More and more, they are tested in essay format with encouragement to find support for unpopular or nonobvious positions. Then, just as they are starting to form their own opinions on subjects from literary interpretation to economics, they are handed a multiple-choice test and told that there is only one correct answer to each question. Parents can make sure this isn't a surprise.

By providing information and stepping back emotionally, you not only allow your child to maintain a lower level of anxiety, but you send the message that you have confidence in your child's ability to master the test. And, should this message take root, it makes your child that much more capable of overcoming anxiety.

We want to raise responsible, self-reliant young people with a realistic view of the world and an optimism in their ability to improve it. This test should neither break their spirits nor define their limits, but should serve as an opportunity for them to learn how to overcome obstacles. In that respect, it's nearly perfect: a predictable, artificial test with real, but not necessarily permanent, consequences. Take advantage of this chance to help your child learn to succeed on her own.

***

Kids are complex creatures and usually more than one stress factor affects test performance. Panicking, choking, and fatigue are three major manifestations of anxiety that we can diagnose and treat, often simultaneously. These three behaviors work together or separately, depending on the individual, to prevent a student from doing his or her best on the day of the test.

Alisa's First Tests
Alisa was a student of average ability and above average anxiety. Wrapped up in a myriad of issues of familial pressure and self-doubt, she often questioned what she was capable of doing. Her practice tests revealed this self-doubt in her abilities, as many of the questions I knew she could answer were scribbled on but the answers were left blank.

While reviewing a diagnostic test on which she had skipped many questions that were, for her, certainly manageable, I asked her to describe what had gone on during the test. She mumbled something about the math being hard and the room being cold.

I then asked her about the students seated near her. She answered offhand that one student next to her seemed intent on breaking the land speed record for completing a diagnostic SAT. How, I asked, did that make her feel? She confessed to feeling that she must have been going "too slow." Each time he turned a page noisily, she assumed that she was falling far behind.

And what about the questions she skipped? "Well," she answered, "I was just taking too long on them, so I had to skip them and move on." "Too long for what?" I asked.

Puzzled, she then recognized that she had abandoned math questions she could answer to move on to other later questions that would predictably be more difficult than she could do. Rather than muttering something to herself about the jerk next to her and simply settling down and finishing the work she had started, she ended up skipping the questions of moderate difficulty in favor of sweating out, and ultimately missing, the highest-level problems.

Alisa had answered about 60 percent of the math questions correctly, muddled about on the next 20 to 30 percent and squandered the rest of her time on the last 10 to 20 percent that she had little chance of getting correct. Pressure, real or perceived, had made her react rather than think.

PANICKING

The vast majority of people panic. They rush. They go too quickly and put themselves in such a state that they simply cannot perform at their highest level. We coach our students in such situations to "read at idiot speed," meaning slow down to the point that you can process the directions word by word and figure it out. Sure, you feel like an idiot for going so slowly but you recognize that, yes, you can in fact do this. On the SAT, the total number of correct answers ultimately matters much more than the number of questions you worked on. By speeding up, Alisa answered several more questions but plummeted in accuracy, and her scores showed it.

Under stress, most people go too fast. They talk too fast, they act without thinking, they deprive themselves of the time needed to do their best. Students, and adults for that matter, can simply think about having to speak in public and they have emotional and physical reactions. People rush their words. They stumble and stammer. The rare individual who can speak in a clear, measured manner seems confident and self-assured. Of course, inside he may be thinking he's talking so slowly that he sounds like an idiot!

And the reason that most people panic, forgetting to do what they know works, is that they lack experience and confidence in the task they are attempting to perform. Think about it: do you panic when you have to merge onto the freeway? Probably not, but the chances are pretty good that you did panic the first time you had to navigate 60 miles-per-hour traffic while accelerating and changing lanes. People don't panic when they know what they're doing.

Now, imagine you're merging into that same stream of traffic, feeling confident because you've done this successfully exactly seven million times before, and you suddenly feel a large snake curl around your legs. Might you feel a bit panicked then? You're in a situation you know well and feel confident about, you have a plan that you are following, and something goes unexpectedly, desperately wrong. You have no experience dealing with this particular driving snafu: what do you do? You panic.

Panic wipes your mind clean, robbing you of the ability to reason your next step. Panic triggers your worst instincts. It increases your heart rate and your breathing, and decreases muscular control. Panic will make you slam on your brakes and swerve your car off the road, regardless of the traffic patterns around you.

What panic won't do is give you the opportunity to recollect the prior events of the day, including the time you offered to drive your son's science project on reptiles to his school. Panic won't let you remember that the insidious monster wrapped around your feet is actually your son's harmless garter snake. Panic only gives you two options: fight or flight. When neither is appropriate, you lose.

Panic on the SAT (hopefully) results in much less calamitous misfortunes, but misfortunes nonetheless. Not being able to think seriously hampers one's ability to read a detailed passage on salmon harvesting in the Pacific Northwest. A blank mind is no help when writing an essay about courage in *The Great Gatsby*. Instincts don't solve geometry problems. No doubt about it, panic is an undesirable outcome when taking the SAT. So why do so many kids seem to set themselves up for it?

First, let's look at why the SAT and panic seem to always travel together. Students take many, many tests over the course of their high school careers, but it seems that the SAT tends to bring out some tendency to panic in just about everyone. From the perfect-scoring math geeks to the kids who are just praying for a passable score, the SAT seems to scare them all. Why does the SAT cause so many people to panic? We are conditioned to fear standardized tests.

Child magazine recently printed an interview with an 11-year-old boy talking about his state's standardized achievement tests. He reported that he was comfortable with the material on the tests, "[b]ut the tests made me nervous. Sometimes kids cry. I've heard of some who have thrown up. There was one girl who was crying with a rosary in her hands and one girl who rubbed her hands so hard they bled."[4] If elementary school children are distressed enough by standardized tests to act in such macabre ways, then it's not hard to see that high school students will be as well.

Part of the reason standardized tests offer such an immediate trigger to panic is their rareness. Kids take hundreds of tests over the course of their education, some more frightening or stressful than others. They take relatively very few standardized tests. The official act of filling out a Scantron answer form and having to sit two seats away from any other student in the cafeteria is nerve-racking, unfamiliar, and uncomfortable.

Another reason standardized tests tend to grip kids in panic is that they offer a ready source of comparison. They're universal; the whole school takes them. If you're lucky, no one outside of your German class needs to know about that last chapter test, but there's no hiding the fact that you did, in fact, just take the SAT. Everyone was there, and everyone saw you.

There's the test itself, of course. The predictor of future success. Harbinger of the good or the bad to come. A high school student's first opportunity to mess up The Rest of His Life. The SAT carries with it an incredible amount of pressure not just because of what it does, which is report your supposed level of academic readiness to colleges, but also because of what it is reputed to do, namely rank you according to level of intelligence. There's just too much at stake to take this particular test calmly.

When you add all of the SAT lore out there to this list, it really starts to add up to a weighty amount of panic. Consider the dinner table discussions about college, the triumphs or failures of older siblings, the high school hallway bragging, and the stern warnings from college counselors. Let's face it—the SAT takes our generalized fear of failure as a society and as individuals and centralizes it in one really long test.

Why Panic Happens

What causes panic is an event that is incongruous with expectations; in other words, something goes wrong, something is different, or something is unfamiliar. It can be as simple as a testing center that is overly air-conditioned. It can be as unpredictable as your ex-boyfriend showing up and sitting in the row ahead of you. Typically, it's an SAT question that just doesn't seem to make sense.

The panic takes over from there. While it's important to try to control the testing environment in order to limit the possibility of a panic-causing distraction, that's often not enough. You just can't predict what might go wrong. You can send your son with an extra sweater and instruct your daughter to keep her head down so she won't see anyone who might upset her, but you can't monitor the proctor to make sure she gives the students their breaks, and you can't control the specific content of the test.

What you can do is make sure that your child knows that things might go wrong. The administration of an SAT is fairly well regulated, but things can go wrong in the most regulated of environments. No vocabulary superstar has seen every word there is. No president of the algebra club can predict what ETS might do with a quadratic equation. Things go wrong, and it happens to everyone. If your child knows this, she'll be less likely to expect a perfect testing day, and therefore less likely to panic when that perfect day doesn't happen.

Because of this, students need tools to deal with the unexpected. They need to plan for something to go wrong, and they need to practice panic. Just as pilot trainees are given mock crashes to deal with in simulators, students need to have a concrete plan of action for when panic takes over. Understanding that things might go wrong helps to prevent panic from happening; having a panic plan helps students overcome a panic episode.

Recognize the Trigger Moment

Because panic manifests itself in an ultimately subtle way—a cessation of rational thought—it can be pretty tough to identify. Students who regularly pause to check their mood and anxiety level stand a better chance of recognizing that something's wrong before panic reaches cataclysmic levels. It's better to be able to say, "Interesting, my pulse is racing and I can't remember what my tutor said to do in this situation," than to just panic.

After a practice test in which things went a bit wrong, teens should try to identify the moment confidence headed south. Often, the answer sheet will reveal the problem's start. One wrong question followed by several more errors signifies panic. A section left unfinished can indicate a distressed state of mind at the beginning of the next section as the student realizes he has fallen behind. A totally complete answer sheet for a student who usually chooses to skip the more difficult questions reveals a panic frame of mind.

Once the moment has been identified, be it during a brief power outage or after a snarly math problem, the student can begin to recognize how, not just when, he lost control. When a student can see in his answer sheet how one measly question or minor incident caused him to blow the whole test, he often trades in anxiety for anger or a greater level of determination. Either reaction is a lot better than anxiety.

Practice, Practice, Practice

Panic is the province of the neophyte. Even though experts have been known to panic, novices are *famous* for it. It makes sense—the more you've done the test, the more comfortable you are with the process. If teens know their method is successful, as Alisa learned, they won't be bothered by Speedy Gonzales over there digging his own grave.

Experts have another skill newcomers lack: they've already tackled bad situations. Things have gone wrong here and there, sometimes terribly, so they've had to deal with a sudden drop in altitude in a twin-engine airplane for instance, or a sentence completion question that just refuses to make sense. They've developed skills for dealing with catastrophe. They've failed before. Parents are generally better drivers than their teens for no other reason than that they have had more experiences with "maniacs" on the road than their children have.

This is why high achievers, especially perfectionists, panic. They don't know that it's OK to "fail." In fact, they are terrified of failing. They've never been there. For high-achieving, perfectionist kids who have high-achieving, perfectionist parents, they simply can't deal with the prospect of "failing." If you can't deal with failure, you can't fix it when it's happening. You also can't learn anything from it.

When panic hits, it's because the brain doesn't know what to do and resorts to fight or flight. If your teen has been in that same situation a few times before, his brain might have a better idea. If he's taken a few practice tests, chances are that he's sat next to a really fast test-taker, a really slow test-taker, and one with a loud, wet cold who forgot to bring tissues and cough drops. His brain is in a better position to acknowledge that conditions aren't optimal but that he can press on.

The story is often told of Edison's many attempts to invent the light bulb. It wasn't so much that Edison got really good at failing but that by the time he had hit upon that perfect filament, he understood why it worked on a deeper level than he could have had he lucked into it on his first try. In fact, this is what Edison had to say about it: "I have not failed. I've just found 10,000 ways that won't work."

Students who are allowed to fail learn more about themselves and the test than those who aren't. Those kinds of learning experiences are just the things you'd like your kid to know before you send him off to college to battle tests that just might matter more.

Treat Underlying Issues

Very few students walk into the SAT without some emotional preconception or pressure. The SAT magnifies insecurities and highlights the most minor and sporadic anxiety. The best time to take care of problems with negative self-image or lowered confidence is before the test—the SAT will only make things worse.

Students who struggle with learning differences have an especially important imperative to focus on their strengths and on success. Students who feel inferior to siblings or classmates must do the same. Most importantly, students who are caught in the confusion of contradictory expectations need to have those clarified in order to overcome anxiety on the test.

Additionally, students who belong to a demographic group that has historically underperformed on tests are in danger of experiencing what experts call stereotype threat. Studies have shown that black students, for instance, will respond to the suggestion that African American students perform poorly on tests by obligingly performing poorly.[5] This works on a micro scale as well, for students who for whatever reason have been labeled poor test-takers.

While we can't always get rid of external pressures, we can teach our kids to recognize them for what they are, and perhaps to learn to put the pressures in the psychic space where they belong. We can give the kids a new message: that they are capable of succeeding on the SAT. After all, we want the tape recording running in their heads during the test to be supporting and encouraging, not sabotaging. And the best way for that to happen is for your child to be free to choose her own thoughts and mantras, not to fall into the default messages of discouragement.

Reframe the Experience and Redefine Success

Panic often occurs because what a student is doing isn't working the way she thinks it should. Maybe nothing in particular has gone wrong, but in her mind the test isn't really going right either. The ensuing feeling of loss of control is usually plenty to trigger a panic episode.

The key here is to take control of the situation. The student can either change the way she's taking the test or change her expectations of the result. Tinkering with these two axes should bring her back to a successful experience. Sometimes expectations are set too high, and sometimes methods need redesigning.

Sometimes kids panic because they missed 1 math question out of 49; this, in their minds, indicates failure. The scoring system of the SAT is partly to blame in its deviation from the tests most high schools give. High school students are trained that at least 90 percent of all questions must be answered correctly in order to achieve a top score. In contrast, on the SAT sometimes answering fewer questions earns a student a higher score, and a student only needs to get roughly two-thirds of the questions correct in order to score well above average. Because the scoring scale is so different on the SAT than on typical high school tests, the SAT tends to addle a student's sense of how success is measured.

Other times, a student's method of proceeding through the test isn't a winner. Some of my students refuse to skip the most difficult and time-consuming questions, thereby squandering the minutes they could better use to complete the easier questions. Other students jump wildly through the test, never sticking with a particular question long enough to ensure accuracy. This usually generates negative results.

By taking the time to analyze why things went wrong, if indeed they did, students can set the stage for more successful experiences the next time around. The goal is to set up an individualized plan for a self-defined success, their way. They win on their terms.

Focus on Process

Panic causes students to obsess about the end results. Students can become so obsessed about the possibility of poor results that they overlook the processes that are the key to great results. Focusing on good processes leads to good end results. Good process is its own reward: You get the positive experience of success while you are testing, as you are successfully sticking to your method. Additionally, you know that doing this will lead to a successful score. Focusing on the process also keeps your mind occupied on productive, correct-answer actions, rather than destructive, scribble-around-desperately actions.

As an additional bonus, when a student really concentrates on the process, he trains his brain to know that route best. Panic is less likely to ensue when a student knows what he is doing and has a plan for when things go wrong. His mind will naturally revert to a practiced plan, and the act of methodically taking action will dissipate panic.

Alisa's Story Continued
I coached Alisa to think of the test in a different way. She was to only answer three-quarters of the questions, spreading the same 25

minutes over 18 or 19 questions rather than 25 questions. I had to show her how the numbers worked out several times in order to get her to believe that her score would actually improve if she answered fewer questions.

When Alisa was able to take a second test in a more measured way, she never even looked at 6 of the 25 questions, which, I assured her, was "perfect." Her score was 90 points higher, for doing less work.

Truth be told, it's not generally too difficult to get many students to acknowledge the wisdom of such an approach. It's getting them to apply it that's the challenge. When doing so, they must pat themselves on the back, remind themselves that letting questions go unanswered is good strategy, not defeat, and feel confident in the knowledge that they are explicitly choosing not to be the proverbial rat feverishly scurrying throughout the maze. By selecting a winning strategy, they not only gain greater control and confidence over the test, but they increase their scores as well.

The real benefit for Alisa, however, was in avoiding a situation that was bound to lead to panic every time. Speeding through the test was, for her, a disastrous idea, and one that was caused by fear and instinct, not by careful focus on the process. By reconstructing the process and giving Alisa successful experiences with it, I was able to show Alisa that all along she had the skills to succeed.

Build Confidence

Students who have repeatedly been told that they can conquer anything that comes their way are much less likely to feel helpless in the face of disaster. Teach your kids that they are capable, and they will be. Tell them not to visualize the test going perfectly; after all, we can't control that crazy proctor or whoever sets the temperature in the testing room. Tell your child to visualize instead responding well to whatever the SAT throws his way that day. We can consistently exercise control over ourselves only, not the circumstances.

Remind your son as he heads out the door to take the SAT that he was really nervous for that physics AP test last month, but that he kept his cool and pulled it off. Let your daughter know that you were proud of her in her last band recital for tackling a tricky song and staying calm and focused during the concert. Give them the priceless gift of your confidence in them.

CHOKING

Every student has a story, and every story is different. Every student also has a different reaction to stress and to the SAT. For most students, understanding the story is the key to helping them write a successful ending. Sometimes the answers spell themselves out on the test itself. Sometimes it's only after talking to the parents that I understand why a student performs the way she does. And sometimes, the SAT isn't the problem at all, but a key to solving the problem. In the following example, we'll look at a specific stress-related reaction to the SAT commonly called *choking*, and some of its manifold causes. We'll continue to present different causes and reactions throughout the book as we discuss solutions, although in some ways the answers are all the same—stay calm, be prepared, be confident. In other ways the uniqueness of each situation can be the most significant factor to consider.

Adrien

Adrien came to see me before the PSAT in his junior year, just as his older brothers had. His two older brothers were All-American athletes and had been accepted to top universities on athletic scholarships. Now, it was Adrien's turn and he had a lot to live up to. With his intensity and determination to succeed, he was a ball of energy and bravado.

Adrien's family was large and close-knit; often, the entire extended family would gather at one of the houses for a family dinner. As aunts, uncles, and cousins sat down to eat together, the same subject arose: the SAT. Adrien was the middle of several cousins close in age, so the subject was of general interest. In this family, the game was numbers, and when PSAT scores came out, Adrien's wasn't high enough. Family dinners became rather painful for Adrien. Session after session he trudged into my office, reporting yet another excruciating family meal. As a result, we spent a lot of time talking about his life and the SAT.

As we worked together, Adrien's knowledge about the SAT increased dramatically, and his skill at solving its problems rose as well.

He completed his SAT homework perfectly and he learned to work quickly. As he began a series of practice tests, I was confident that Adrien was better prepared to earn a higher score. But Adrien's scores didn't improve. Something else was factoring in to Adrien's test-taking experience.

You have probably already guessed part of what was going on when Adrien sat down to take a practice test. Some of the commonalities are all too apparent in Adrien's case: extreme family pressure, a history of trying to "measure up," and low self-confidence. Adrien's particular testing reaction, however, is harder to identify.

As soon as the proctor announced the start time on a practice test, Adrien's mind went into hyperdrive. It was as if he had suddenly forgotten everything he knew about the SAT. The simplest questions seemed sinister, hiding tricks for the unwary. The harder questions seemed impossible. Overthinking everything, Adrien didn't dare to skip any steps or rely on his intuition. He slowed to a crawling pace and sweated over every calculation. He emerged hours later, exhausted, and would hand me a test scribbled throughout with notes: "I can't do this!" and "What is happening?!?" followed by, "I think I failed this section!" A couple of times he gave up partway through the test, unable emotionally to go on.

I went over the tests with Adrien, and in nearly every instance, he was able to quickly point out his errors. He couldn't believe the incorrect answers he'd chosen. Instead of making him feel better, however, this just reinforced the idea in his mind that test-taking was something he just wasn't good at. Rather than seeing his test-taking behavior as a temporary obstacle, he believed that his cousins were right, and he could never improve. His perception was that what happened to him during the test was not understandable or controllable.

Adrien's natural response to stress is in fact fairly common. Slowing down, overthinking simple steps, and a fear of mistakes that leads to a rejection of intuition and instinct—this set of behaviors is sometimes called choking. Think of a baseball player too stressed to feel natural at the plate, or a surfer who isn't "in the zone." To perform, even something you're really good at, requires that you trust in your ability. Choking was Adrien's natural response to stress: the more stressed he felt, the worse he performed.

Psychologists differentiate between *explicit* and *implicit* learning. Again, sports analogies usually work best to explain this difference. Think of explicit learning as a very conscious and sequential approach to, say, basketball: dribble down the court, take two steps, and toss the ball up right-handed for a lay-up. Sure, that's how anyone would begin to learn to play the game. At a certain point, though, the process becomes more complicated and more fluid as well as less conscious. The player is now dodging opponents, negotiating a sweat-slicked floor, and favoring a strained ankle while performing the same task *without* counting out the steps sequentially. Instead of taking every action explicitly, overtly, and consciously, the basketball player is implicitly acting and increasing in skill and ability. His well-trained instincts now guide his lay-up.

The two actions described above are handled in two separate areas of the brain; first the conscious and sequential learning and action of a lay-up occurs in one section of the brain, and as the athlete increases in experience and skill, another portion of the brain guides his improved and more instinctual lay-ups. It's not just a matter of doing it better; it's doing it differently. When stressed, an athlete prone to choking will allow the explicit system to take over, slowing down and reverting to step-by-step game-play. As if he were a beginner, he will count his steps and deliberate over his arm movements. He'll lose his ability to play the game fluidly, easily, and instinctively.

Students taking a test experience the same phenomenon when they choke. They'll shut down the implicit portion of their brains and revert to analyzing even the simplest problems. In that way, choking is not a form of panic, but the opposite of panic. People who panic revert to instinct rather than rational thought. People who choke lose their instincts and think too much.[6]

Because these two reactions are so different, the conventional wisdom regarding panic on tests—slow down, take a deep breath, work harder, practice more, take this more seriously—are wildly unsuccessful in a choking situation. Working harder won't increase a student's ability to rely on his instincts when it matters. As Adrien demonstrated, the harder a choker works, the more stressful the moment of performance becomes, and the worse he chokes.

For any timed test, choking is bad news—it robs you of the ability to quickly work through questions, to trust your instincts, and to take

advantage of your specialized test knowledge. For the SAT, choking can
be disastrous.

*Marcel came to work with me the fall of his junior year. A bright
guy, Marcel had worked his sophomore year with a highly regarded
and experienced tutor in the area. I wondered what could be the
source of Marcel's underperformance.*

*Like many students, Marcel was gunning for scores that started
with a seven. His actual scores the previous spring had been 660 on
both the math and verbal portions of the old SAT. I asked about
practice tests and learned his scores on those had ranged from the
mid-600 range of his actual scores to the low 700s he sought. His
processes looked solid. We tweaked a few things but nothing looked
terribly awry. I sent him home to do a practice test with instructions
to do the test at his own pace, to really nail his processes, but to watch
his time.*

*The next week, he presented me his test with scores of 730 math
and 720 verbal. "Fantastic," I said, "So how long did it take?"
"About 45 minutes a section." The given time for those sections was
30 minutes a section. Okay. If Marcel had all the time in the world,
he'd do just fine. Unfortunately, we had to find a way to get him to
do just fine in a third less time.*

*I gave him something equivalent to the following question: If
$x \geq 0$, and $(x-2)^2 = 25$, what is x? Now, if you have not done math in
the last two decades, you are more than forgiven for not knowing how
to do this. For students in high school, this should generally be a relatively easy question. What Marcel did was the following:*

$$(x-2)\,(x-2) = 25$$
$$x^2 - 2x - 2x + 4 = 25$$
$$x^2 - 4x + 4 = 25$$
$$x^2 - 4x - 21 = 0$$

*He then looked at the above, determined he wasn't sure how to
factor it, and applied the quadratic equation:*

$$x = \frac{-b \pm \sqrt{(b^2 - 4ac)}}{2a}$$

$$a = 1,\, b = -4,\, c = -21$$

Plugging in the values from his equation gave him:

$$x = \frac{4 \pm \sqrt{(16 - -84)}}{2}$$

$$x = \frac{4 \pm \sqrt{100}}{2}$$

$$x = \frac{4 \pm 10}{2}$$

This gave him two possible values for x, 7 and –3. As the problem specified that x was greater than zero, Marcel chose the answer 7, and thereby finished the problem. Whew. Marcel's solution to this math problem was perfectly correct. His math teacher would have been proud. I was alarmed. It had taken him four-and-a-half minutes.

I said, "Is there a quicker way to do that?" Marcel looked surprised, and then thought. "Well," he said after a moment, "I guess the inside of the parentheses would need to equal 5, since 5 squared equals 25. So, x would equal 7, since 7 minus 2 equals 5. That's it, x equals 7." Indeed, more than a step or two quicker.

I pointed out to Marcel that this problem was similar to the very first problem on another practice test. I stated to Marcel my sincere belief that his skills were excellent, that he was bright and had been taught very well by his previous tutor. I then gave him another test with different instructions. He was to do this test as fast as he possibly could, without doing anything exceptionally stupid, that is.

A week later he returned with his retest. Scores? Math 720 and verbal 700. Statistically the same as his previous test. The time? Twenty to 25 minutes per section. Wow.

Under pressure, those who choke revert to being beginners. They do each and every step with utter deliberation. They lose faith in their intuition. It's akin to athletes who are thinking about their swing or their shot rather than just hitting the ball or making the shot. The Nike slogan "Just do it" is apt advice. By telling Marcel to simply go as fast as he could, I gave him permission to "run," to just do it, without thinking about the consequences.

Fortunately, choking is just one of the many normal and controllable reactions to stress. For Adrien, the solution was different from

Marcel's solution. Once Adrien began to understand what his mind was doing and why, he began to feel more control over the situation. We picked apart his practice test experience, discussing how he felt at each stage of the exam. He started to identify what was happening during each phase, and to understand why his errors were so easy for him to correct later. We talked about *how* this happens and *why* this happens.

We then learned to pinpoint the onset of the stress. In short drills, we introduced stress to Adrien at increasing levels until he was able to recognize the "trigger moment" when his composure and testing ability began to be threatened. Simply recognizing the onset of his reactions helped him to understand how he was allowing his emotions to affect him. Adrien could feel the change, from relying on his intuition and skill to focusing on his insecurity.

Finally, we gave Adrien tools to combat the stress. In practice tests, he no longer focused on the questions but on his heart rate and sense of control. When he felt a "trigger moment" arise, Adrien would pause, breathe slowly in and out, and repeat a series of affirmations until he felt calm enough to continue. Even an exercise as simple as this was enough for him to take the focus away from the stress and place it on something more controllable: his respiration in this case, or a practice mantra of assurance. For Adrien, this was enough to allow him to perform without choking.

For other students, a variety of techniques have proven more effective. Some need to build up a backlog of successful testing experiences to fight the negative feelings that swamp them. Others write a short reminder on the top of each page of the test, asserting control and calm each time they turn a page. I've had some students surround themselves with a sturdy structure of routine: they use the same pencil, sit in the same desk, repeat the same mnemonics, and follow the same fixed methods on the problems. When choking threatens to cause them to forget all they know about the test, often following the sheer routine of the situation can get them back on track before they're too far gone.

Just because your child is experiencing anxiety on the test, he's not necessarily panicking. Giving him more practice tests, instructing him to slow down and concentrate more, or offering another pep talk may not be the prescription your son needs. Pay attention to the clues and cues that will reveal just what is happening when your son takes an SAT. The path his anxiety takes may surprise you, and you may need to rethink the ways that you help him deal with his stress and underperformance.

Adrien's Story Continued

Choking itself was not Adrien's problem. Choking was just the manifestation of Adrien's problem. What happened to Adrien during the test stemmed from a variety of sources and combined to make him feel more insecure during a period of his life already fraught with insecurity. His brothers' well-meaning suggestions only served as reminders of his feelings of inadequacy. His cousins' bluffing confidence made him feel that he was the only one who had to work hard for his scores. Adrien's parents inadvertently added to his concerns by suggesting more practice tests and more homework. Adrien worked harder, adding pressure to himself and more anxiety to his test taking. The harder he worked, the more emotional and spectacular were his failures.

As time went by, Adrien became more emotional, more unstable in his personal relationships, and quite uncertain about the future. Not surprisingly, his practice test scores hovered somewhat below his ability level. Seen from this angle, the SAT was no longer the problem; it was a lens through which to see the problem.

As we worked on Adrien's choking, he began to look more seriously at the external factors that were influencing his view of the SAT. He recognized his underperformance and knew there was something wrong not just with his testing, but with the intensity the SAT had for him. As the problem worsened, his recognition of the problem grew.

For Adrien, the key to combating the hideous hold the SAT had on his life was to reframe its meaning and importance. Adrien began to question his personal goals, and found that they did not always align with his parents' expectations or his older brothers' examples. He discovered that he was looking for a more laid-back college than the East Coast schools his brothers attended, and that he wasn't sure he wanted to play sports. He began to reevaluate his career goals and to seek college programs that would help him realize those goals. Once Adrien had carved out his own vision of his life, he was able to some extent to take the numbers, and the stress, out of the game.

For Adrien and for most other students, the causes and the symptoms reinforced each other to increase the problem. The reverse is also true: as Adrien learned to combat choking, he gained more confidence. As he grew more confident, the choking became less of a problem. Not surprisingly, his score jumped above his target range.

Interestingly, Adrien ultimately chose to take the same path his brothers had, accepting an athletic scholarship to a prestigious university near his home. For him, conquering the SAT had given him the power to choose, instead of simply conforming or rebelling. When Adrien entered college that fall, he took with him more than just a great SAT score: Adrien brought self-confidence and self-awareness into his freshman year of college when he needed it most.

FATIGUE

Main Entry: fa·tigue
Pronunciation: fə-'tēg
Function: *noun*
Etymology: French, from Middle French, from *fatiguer* to fatigue, from Latin *fatigare*; akin to Latin af*fatim* sufficiently
1 a : LABOR b : manual or menial work performed by military personnel c *plural* : the uniform or work clothing worn on fatigue and in the field
2 a : weariness or exhaustion from labor, exertion, or stress b : the temporary loss of power to respond induced in a sensory receptor or motor end organ by continued stimulation
3 : the tendency of a material to break under repeated stress[7]

The SAT specializes in catching a student with a secondary or tertiary meaning of a word. Knowing a vocabulary word isn't enough—you also need to know little-used meanings, usages that have fallen out of fashion, and sometimes even the etymology of an obscure word. And as in the word *fatigue*, above, sometimes understanding all the meanings and how they work together is required to answer correctly.

The new SAT might just be an elaborate psychological experiment testing the effects of the various meanings of *fatigue* on the teenage brain and body. Not only has the·length of the test itself dramatically increased, the span of time over which SAT anxiety is likely to prevail has stretched as well. It used to be that the junior year PSAT announced the beginning of the SAT season, with most students taking the test during the fall of their senior year. Now, sophomores and often freshman routinely take the PSAT. Some schools administer a PSAT in seventh grade, although its predictive value at that point is, predictably, quite low. More students are taking the SAT earlier as well—the spring of their junior year or even December or January of their junior year, nearly two full years before they expect to enroll in college. There's even an unfortunate trend among some sophomores to get their first SAT out of the way before they've even taken the official PSAT in the fall of their junior year.

To keep up with the increased anxiety, more and more students are asking to start working with a tutor during their sophomore year and earlier. The SAT has expanded to color a student's entire high school experience. Talk about test fatigue—you don't have to be an SAT tutor to get thoroughly sick of hearing about this test.

To return to the favorite subject of SAT critics, the length of the test itself has radically altered the test-taking experience for high school students, as well as the demographic of those whose scores excel. This test no longer rewards the cleverest and fastest students with the best vocabulary. It now rewards the cleverest and fastest students with the best vocabulary who also happen to have remarkable powers of endurance and focus, and who incidentally typically get at least eight hours of sleep per night. That's a smaller group and not necessarily a better group to reward.

For most students, all the definitions of *fatigue* will forcibly come into play during the test. I tell my students that they are soldiers, using strategy to fight against ETS and their own anxiety. They combat weariness of body, exhaustion of mind, and the physical symptoms of sleep deprivation robbing their synapses of their typical speed. They are also fighting the tendency of their own psyches to break under the repeated stress of the high school standardized testing regimen.

Wake Up

Check your child's SAT entrance ticket to find out when he's supposed to show up. It's much earlier than it used to be. ETS now instructs everyone to arrive by 7:45 AM, not between 8:15 and 8:30 AM, as in the past. The test starts earlier because it's much longer. If you get the students out of there by about 1:00 PM, the fact that they were being tested for five hours won't be as noticeable. After all, one o'clock is a great time for lunch.

With such an early wake-up call, students have a tendency to sleep as late as possible so they'll be more rested, then roll out of bed and into the testing room just before the test starts. Unfortunately, it takes much more than a couple of minutes for the brain to wake up and start performing optimally. The research varies, but most scientists agree that you're not working at your peak first thing in the morning.

Studies suggest that peoples' brains really aren't awake for about an hour and a half after they wake up. For teenagers with their growth spurts and routine sleep deprivation, that time until their brains get in gear might conceivably be three or four hours. It's a good idea to get them up early enough before the test to do either a reading passage or read a newspaper to get the verbal part of the brain awake. Encourage them to run a half mile, or at least around the block, to get the blood moving. Protein for breakfast also speeds the wake-up process.

But for kids who are just lethargic by habit for the first several hours of the morning, they need to do something extra to not have that be their state at the beginning of the SAT. Much in the same way that you don't just put on your cleats and jump right into a soccer game, but instead jog around and kick the ball a bit before you get started, it's a good idea to go over stuff you've already done well to get your head around the test and get engaged in the testing process.

One of my students, Jamal, was never awake. He slogged into every tutoring session. At his parents' request, I met with him for half an hour on the morning of the SAT to get him engaged and review his game plan one more time before he left to take the test. That morning his brain seemed to be impervious to all the last-minute advice that I wanted to give him.

I tried all I could do to wake that kid up, but his droopy eyes told me it wasn't working. So I finally closed his book and looked at him and said, "Jamal, you know this stuff, you've done tons of practice. You just need to be awake and you're not awake." I then told him to get in his car, roll the windows all the way down and crank the stereo all the way up, and drive with semi-abandon all the way to the test. For the first time that morning, his eyes lit up and he answered me, "OK!" I heard the tires squeal as he drove away, the bass sounds from his stereo radiating through the neighborhood. I crossed my fingers. No speeding ticket, I prayed. But hey, that might help wake him up, too.

When the SAT started a few minutes later, he was awake; he was ready; he crushed the test.

Anxiety and Fatigue

What is attributed to garden variety test anxiety is most often a combination of an imperfect command of the subject matter and the natural effects of sleep deprivation: you don't know the stuff that well, you can't recall it that well, and you get easily upset and frustrated because you're tired. For most students, one of the reasons they fall victim to anxiety is that they are simply too tired to deal with the test material properly.

It's an easy habit for people to fall into. They stay up too late, so they're tired during the day, and they don't learn the material in their classes. To prepare for a quiz or a test they have to start over to learn what they would have known had they been awake during class. So they stay up really late preparing because they're not reviewing—they're trying to really learn the stuff for the first time. The next day, because they've learned this information in a slapdash and hurried way, they can easily find the quiz or test difficult since the information is jumbled instead of organized in their heads. Learning is like building with bricks: lay some down, let them set, then lay down more. Finally, since they've stayed up all night preparing for this quiz or test, their time spent in other classes is wasted as well because they are too tired to really absorb new information. And the cycle continues.

It's important for students to be able to see what is making them feel the way they feel, and what is limiting their abilities to perform the way they'd like to. It's hard to do triage as an adolescent; it's hard to know when you can stop and take some time to recover and reassess. If we can help our kids not only to see the pattern of stress and sleep deprivation in their lives, but also to take control of their schedules and bedtimes, we've given them a chance to take control of the SAT as well.

Sleep Deprivation

Sleep research indicates that the first two things to go when a person is sleep deprived are emotional control and verbal recall.[8] Emotional control really comes in handy when you're trying to deal with the stress and anxiety of a major test. What about verbal recall? My students tell me that it's helpful too, at least on the critical reading and writing sections of the test.

Students can check on the emotional control part by how stressed they feel. I ask my students if they've ever noticed that their moms are always a pain in the neck when they're tired. "Oh yeah," they say, "why is it she always gives me a hard time when I'm really worn out?!" When little frustrations become big problems, maybe a nice long nap is in order. When a bizarre-looking vocabulary word makes you want to cry, perhaps you're just tired.

Verbal recall is the equivalent of the little guy who is supposed to walk to the back of your brain and open the filing cabinet to get the word or answer you want. When you're sleep deprived, he seems to be on a permanent coffee break. Whether it's writing an essay, figuring out a sentence completion question, or piercing through a tough reading passage, that little guy is going to be essential.

One of my students, Kim, complained that her sleep deprivation was a result of insomnia. I just couldn't accept that an otherwise healthy teenager was simply unable to sleep at night, so I delved deeper. She claimed that she would go to bed at a reasonable time, say 11 PM, but then would lie in bed for hours, unable to fall asleep. I asked her about medications she was taking—nope. I asked her about exercise patterns, napping, and emotional anxiety—nope. I then started picking apart the course of a normal day for her.

Kim walked me through her whole afternoon and evening. It was typical stuff—calling friends, doing homework, watching a little TV. She then revealed, "Well, at some point I eat a snack." What kind of snack? "A drink or something like that." What kind of drink? Well, as it turns out, this girl had a minifridge in her room, and every evening around 10:30 PM she would drink a Diet Coke. Heading off to bed not long after, she would understandably struggle to fall asleep, having unwittingly caffeinated herself into alertness. How about some water or a nice glass of milk instead?

Among all the sleep-deprived groups in America, teens are the blue-ribbon winners. Needing on average 8 ½ to 9 ¼ hours of sleep per night, in reality they get fewer than 7 hours per night by the end of high school.[9] Let's face it—most of our kids are just plain tired.

A 1996 study by the Center for Applied Research and Educational Improvement (CAREI) at the University of Minnesota[10] took a close look at school start times as a way of increasing the alertness of students during school hours. Their results were surprising. When school moved from a start time of 7:45 AM to 8:30 AM, the students all got one hour more sleep per night. That's right—their bedtimes did not change; they just slept later.

The other results were also somewhat surprising, in their scope. Attendance and continuous enrollment went up. Tardiness, trips to the principal's office, and trips to the school nurse went down. More kids ate breakfast and completed homework during school hours. Students were more attentive, and the atmosphere in the schools was calmer and more controlled. The school counselors reported that fewer students sought help for stress relief and problems with their peers and parents.

For a lot of kids, the pressure of performing in a highly competitive environment such as high school is both the cause and the result of not enough sleep. For many kids, sports practices added to hours of homework per night added to testing anxiety equals late nights studying and few and fitful hours of sleep. For today's high achieving kids, top GPAs and test scores aren't enough—parents and colleges expect excellence in sports, music, and other arenas. Some of these kids might need to reassess priorities and cut down on commitments. Others just need a bit of help dealing with the stress. Sometimes these kids appear so independent and adult that we forget they often don't have access to adult-level stress management skills. We expect them to cope better than our adult population at large does.

The truth is that many teenage sleep deprivation problems are actually solvable. Just by adding a half hour of sleep per night, a student can dramatically increase his sleep bank. That's one less sitcom rerun, or just dropping the habit of checking e-mail one last time before bed. Just doing that, and even just doing that the week before the SAT, adds up to points on the test.

I plead with my students, telling them that if I could get them to do only one thing the week of the test, it's go to bed early the whole week. It's not the night before the marathon that runners hit the sack early—it's the night before the night before. Calling the evening quits at 8 PM the night before the test just won't work on its own. Besides, a body used to an 11 PM bedtime probably won't comply.

In some way, the reason we enjoy holidays and pine for them as a period of contentment and joy is that during holidays, you get to be completely rested. You get to stay up late and do neat things without getting punished for it the next morning. In some ways, sleeping in is the real holiday, the real cause for celebration.

While we probably won't get all the high schools in America to move to a 10 AM start time before the next SAT, we can make life a bit less punishing for our teenagers. We can build in more buffer time in their schedules; we can unpack their lists of commitments a bit; we can encourage good sleep habits. We can also switch off those lights just a half hour earlier, giving them the support they need to make sleep a priority. After all, we want them to be their best not just on the day of the SAT, but at all times. On the day of the SAT, if they have just that little bit of extra energy to check their math calculations, to be creative in the essay, or to read that passage with a bit more focus, they might just earn the scores that they really deserve.

CHAPTER SIX

Disincentives to Success

The SAT is the first real-life test most kids take. We know how this test is different from other high school tests. We know what the scores mean, and how they are used by college admissions committees. What we don't always understand is how this one test colors and informs a teenager's progression to college and adulthood. In the spring of their junior year, 15- to 16-year-olds are given a test that is not only structured unlike tests they've seen before, but has consequences much heavier than anything they've done before. This isn't a sophomore year third-quarter geometry final—it's a score that will be sent to colleges to aid them in determining whether an aspiring scientist will get to achieve his dream of attending Cal Tech. The way kids react to the SAT is in a large part a reflection of the pressure they feel associated with the test.

Psychologists are fond of telling us that all behaviors have payoffs. Studying hard gives you great grades, while not studying hard gives you more free time. Dieting and exercising make your body feel and look good, while eating a carton of ice cream on the couch while watching M*A*S*H reruns is relaxing and tastes great.

Try telling that to the parent of a teenager who repeatedly panics on tests. What's the payoff there? Why would a child risk his future by indulging in behaviors that have always proved unsuccessful? Well, the truth of the matter is that on some level, some payoff is happening. For most kids, those whose anxiety difficulties don't reach the clinical level, there is some reward somewhere for panicking on standardized tests. There are incentives to keep kids repeating the same testing mistakes and just as many, or more, deterrents to change that behavior. This is a critical component of SAT preparedness—not only understanding what is motivating the undesired behavior, but knowing how to actually alter the incentive structure such that poor testing behavior is no longer worthwhile to the student.

Changing a student's attitude toward a test is simply a matter of removing disincentives to success while providing incentives to success. Sound too easy? Let's tackle the disincentives first, and some of them will be surprising. When I first began tutoring years ago, I puzzled over the reluctance some of my students had to admitting their successes. We'd increase scores by hundreds of points and my students would still mutter, "That was a fluke, I'm not really that good at testing," or "Yeah, but the reading passages were really easy on that test," or "I still missed that math question that I should have gotten right." This isn't all poor self-image talking. For some reason, these kids were hesitant to accept the role of a successful test-taker.

I'll give you an example to start us on the road to discovering what types of disincentives are plaguing many high school students. Take a look at this test case, and see if you can find the pattern of behavior:

I tutored Amanda for the SAT when she was a junior in high school. Amanda was high stress all the way. She was self-disparaging to the point that I suspected her of sabotaging her homework to convince me of her ineptitude. Yet Amanda was desperately ambitious and worked harder than most students I've seen. She wanted to attend a top college—it seemed like she had every incentive in the world to succeed.

Every method I taught Amanda, she grabbed hold of as if it was a life preserver. Faithfully applying techniques, she would often take circuitous routes to apply complex methods to the simplest of problems. Rather than just working out the answer to a math problem, she would laboriously recall each step of the methods I had taught her, even when she knew the answer from the beginning. I taught her everything she needed to know for the test, and gave her one last pep talk at our final appointment.

Late the night before the SAT, my cell phone rang. It was Amanda, and she was hysterical. "I'm freaking out already! I can't do this, I can't do this. What should I do? Help me!" I spent the next half hour reassuring Amanda, reminding her of her practice test successes, of the improvement she'd shown, and of how much she knew.

Amanda did fine on the SAT, but not quite as well as her practice tests showed she could. Five years later, I tutored Amanda for the LSAT. Amanda had previously attended a large LSAT prep course and had learned detailed and bulky methods for each particular part of the LSAT. The bulky methods, she could handle. What she could not do, however, was determine what type of problem was in front of her in order to select the appropriate method. She also couldn't finish enough of the test in the time allotted to get a good score. I slowly started removing the procedural crutches Amanda was using, and discovered something a bit surprising: Amanda was really good at the LSAT. Not the methods, not the tricky techniques, but the actual logic of the LSAT.

Over the course of a few sessions, I helped Amanda complete LSAT sections quickly and accurately, without the smothering methods. It was a slow process, as Amanda was extremely reluctant to part with the methods that were clearly holding her back. I then began questioning Amanda about her level of anxiety. Amanda responded instantly, with a degree of self-satisfaction: "I'm horrible at tests. I always freak out. Don't you remember how I had to call you the night before the SAT because I was such a basket case?" For Amanda, preparing for the LSAT wouldn't be so much a matter of mastering the material on the test—she was already well on her way—but more a matter of letting go of the benefits she had received in the past as a result of her particular brand of anxiety.

For five years, Amanda had held on to a behavior that negatively affected her academic success. For five years, she chose to not alter the pattern that had carried her through the SAT. In five years of school, Amanda had not replaced the story of her testing behavior, a story written during or before her junior year SAT. After graduating from a prestigious university with her bachelor's degree, Amanda's testing experience was still epitomized by a panic attack before the SAT. Nothing in between mattered—not eight consecutive semesters peppered with quizzes and tests and culminating in lengthy and challenging finals. Amanda was a bad test-taker because she had decided to be so during her junior year of high school. She had reaped some benefit for doing so and was not ready to let that benefit go.

There's another hint in this story to help uncover Amanda's disincentives to do well on the LSAT. She was actually, on some level, almost proud of her panic attack, way back five years earlier, the night before the SAT.

Let's dissect further these two interrelated phenomena that we've briefly outlined: developing an interest in being "a bad test-taker," and adopting a "testing personality" early on in life and sticking to it. We'll do this by pestering Amanda a little bit longer, using her story to uncover relevant facts. Keep in mind that Amanda was a hard worker, a smart girl from a supportive family who was successful in all other areas of her academic life. This is by no means an indictment of Amanda, but rather an attempt to discover what can be hindering teenagers from overcoming testing anxiety.

Amanda came from a family that valued academic and professional achievement and had known for years that her path in life would involve a prestigious university education. Standardized tests were a problem; Amanda wasn't naturally good at them. She knew, also, that this was a problem her parents couldn't fix. The SAT rests squarely on the shoulders of the kids who take it, and no amount of blaming bad teachers will excuse a poor score. In fact, there's usually no *one* at all to blame.

Amanda, like many others, was resourceful enough to find some-*thing* to blame. She was overwhelmed by the pressure associated with this test and desired so intensely to please her parents and prove her worth. Naturally, all this anxiety led Amanda to feel panicked and to latch on to this emotion. After the SAT, she could feel proud of how well she did despite her minor panic attack. She could also explain to others when reporting her score that she had performed very well for someone practically disabled by her unfortunate condition. She undoubtedly heard her parents repeat the story: "Poor thing, Amanda's always really stressed for major exams."

It's not too hard to see where this is going. Increased parental attention, increased peer group attention, and even some institutional attention are all disincentives for Amanda to change the situation. For some kids, extra tutoring comes next, complete with thorough discussion of the problem and further validation of the condition. Some kids receive therapy to help them overcome their anxiety. Within the peer group, and especially in the social world of young girls, panicking on tests seems to be not only a legitimate behavior, but also carries a measure of cachet. It can help teenagers identify themselves within a group, and they enjoy that solidarity.

Take a look Table 6.1 for some of the disincentives that may be operating on your child. Dissecting these ideas one by one can help to identify what factors may or may not be in play, and therefore what incentives need to be altered.

It's important to understand as we examine these disincentives that virtually no child recognizes or admits that he's responding to subtle messages telling him to fail. This response isn't overt on the part of the child; it isn't even conscious. Think of it in terms of your commute to work. Suppose there's a direct route, just a few miles long, that would take you right to the front door of your office. Every time you take that route, however, you get rerouted by construction detours, get stuck behind a school bus that makes stops on every corner, or get lost in a particularly tricky section of town. That route is also lined with speed traps and is generally crowded with unusually aggressive drivers who routinely shout obscenities at you as you try to maneuver around them. It doesn't make sense to go that way, does it? The other route takes a few minutes longer but lets you arrive at work much less harried. That's what's happening, on a less-than-conscious level, to your child. His goal isn't to drive you crazy or to ruin his chances of getting into college: his goal is self-preservation. He's choosing a process that makes sense to him given what he sees on his road—his experiences at school

Table 6.1

Common Disincentives

---

1. Parental attention
2. Institutional attention
3. Identity within a group
4. Perceptions of control
5. Taking responsibility (or not)
6. Self-image
7. Fear

---

and on the test. It may not make much sense to you as his parent, but then you're using a different map.

PARENTAL ATTENTION

This is a familiar dynamic from infants to adults. For some reason, we like negative attention from our parents. The stock reason is that negative attention is better than no attention at all, although that doesn't always tell the whole story. It is the whole story for those students who really can perform well in stressful situations, such as the SAT, and are simply trying to receive some recognition from their parents for their abilities and successes. It can be frustrating to be the honor roll kid whose parents pay no attention to her hard work, and it can be difficult to muster up the self-discipline to keep working that hard if it seems that no one cares. Flubbing the SAT is a great way to say, "Hey, look at me! This isn't so easy, you know!" For these kids, removing the disincentive is as easy as providing more recognition for the hard work they do.

For many other kids, sometimes their continued testing anxiety is at some level trying to communicate to their parents that they need help. They're worried about the test, they're fearful about the consequences of the test, and they're not ready to be adults yet. Adulthood is coming on fast, and it can be a scary thing. The SAT is a very tangible reminder that real life is approaching, and kids know that if they mess up on the SAT, they're messing up their futures. While expressing that fear openly isn't always easy for teens, there are other ways to get the message across. Letting these emotions loose on the test usually does the trick.

When these emotions translate into testing anxiety, often a teenager will receive immediate and palpable assistance. The problem of the SAT moves from a personal problem to a shared family problem, and some of the anxiety can dissipate right there. The student no longer has to feel alone on his first foray into the adult world—he's got his parents right there with him, just as concerned and involved as he is. When parents become involved, the child can then either express his concerns, or, more commonly, wait for his parents to discover and fix them.

How do you remove this disincentive? Be involved in your child's SAT preparations. Help her choose how to prepare for the SAT. Make sure she understands how the test works. Take some of the responsibility for planning for and prepping for this test. Your child may not thank you, but you've removed one obstacle from her path. If she doesn't want help, tell her that you respect her independence, you have confidence in her ability to prepare for this test, and that you've looked into some test preparation options for her to choose from.

INSTITUTIONAL ATTENTION

If the problem is deemed serious enough, a teenager's parents may seek solutions outside of the family. Parents might talk to their child's teachers about the problem, or research books or websites. The child might be sent to classes, to a tutor, or to a therapist to help work through the anxiety and testing difficulties. In all of those options, this teenager is receiving increased attention from important people. He's being asked what he thinks; his concerns are being listened to and taken seriously. In many cases, high school students I've tutored have eagerly confided in me their fears and concerns, and turned to me with their anxieties, looking for validation and support.

Remember Amanda? Remember the phone call, the night before the test? Amanda valued having a trusted relationship with me and appreciated the feeling that when she felt unsure, she had someone knowledgeable she could turn to, someone who knew her and cared about her problems. For a teenager about to take the SAT, that's a significant value.

First, make sure your child is receiving some kind of individual attention in his SAT preparation. If he's prepping at home with books and other materials, check in with him. Offer to grade his practice tests and quiz him on vocabulary. Help him understand why he missed the problems he missed, and help him develop an individualized timing and skipping strategy. Don't let your child feel that he's in this alone.

If your child is prepping in a group class, make sure she stays after to ask the teacher her specific questions. See if the teacher will spend a few extra minutes looking at your child's progress and making recommendations. With most classes, you can also pay for extra tutor time with that teacher to ensure that your child is getting the attention she needs to feel secure. If this isn't an option for you, ask your child's high school teachers to spend a little time with your child to help address her concerns. If your child is prepping with a tutor, ask the tutor about your child's specific learning and testing styles, and how the material is being modified to suit her individual needs. Also, make sure that your child feels comfortable asking her tutor questions and getting feedback.

Second, if your child has already experienced a major anxiety-related episode, sit down with him and talk to him about it. Listen to his concerns first and then explain that anxiety is a very common reaction to stressful situations, and that you have confidence that together you'll find the way to overcome this problem. Share experiences from your life when you overcame anxiety, and then remind your child of his own past experiences quelling anxiety in different situations. Then present some options for dealing with the problem and ask your child for his input as to how to proceed. This will empower your child and help him understand that not only *can* he conquer his anxiety, but that ultimately he is the only one who can.

IDENTITY WITHIN A GROUP

The demographics of competition within the typical American high school are a marvelous thing. The majority of the students I've tutored based their target scores on the median range of their social subset. In other words, what their friends got on the test is what they want to get on the test. And to an alarming degree, those friends are getting remarkably similar scores. Naturally, much of this is perception distortion—a student will know three people who did well and immediately extrapolate that the *entire school* got above 2100 on the SAT. Additionally, the chances are pretty high that at least one, and possibly all three, of those high scorers is lying about her score. Of course, no one believes that her friends would lie about this, and so to avoid the humiliation of being the *only person* at the school who didn't score above 2100, the student is practically forced to also lie about her own score, and the cycle continues.

Regardless of the truth of the situation, most of my students are judging their test scores based on their peers' test scores, who are also judging their test scores on each other's. Never mind that the colleges won't care if Cindy did better than Rachel who did better than Melinda—this is how teenagers can make sense of a scoring system that makes no sense to them when they have no idea how colleges use it.

Testing personalities go right along with this behavior: if your friends are all stressed, you're stressed, too. It's just good manners. If your daughter's friends panic, chances are good that your daughter will too. It still doesn't usually pay in the typical American high school to stick out too far. And don't forget, since your daughter is getting most of her test information from her peers, she's likely to believe pretty much anything they say.

The opposite situation occurs perhaps even more frequently. When a student has a score substantially below the perceived social group median, a panic attack can neatly explain the discrepancy. The suffering student can therefore keep her status as an intelligent member of the group while adding the often-valuable distinction of being high strung, or emotional, or just plain anxious on tests.

While this particular social phenomenon seems to be much more common with girls, high school boys typically have their own corollary. With some boys, working too hard or studying too much can be a social liability, as can taking a test too seriously. Getting a fabulous SAT score is great if you do it with no effort. Working really hard and still not doing well lands a boy in the same sticky spot as that girl whose score was embarrassingly below her peer group's range. We see many of those boys claiming a lack of interest in the test or a generalized inability to focus. These trends change, as peer groups and the social reality change, so watch for variations in your child's behavior.

The problem with these test-score-explanation behaviors is that they generate negative testing outcomes. After all, if panicking is your excuse, or not caring, or not being able to focus, then you've got to feed into that to make it believable. More importantly, to the student, it usually *is* believable. And that's how it becomes a disincentive. If you believe that you can't focus on tests (and you believe that because your score came out lower than you thought it should have), then you have a pretty strong disincentive to prepare for those tests. Why know everything if you can't concentrate long enough to put that knowledge to use? During the test, why try to concentrate more if you know deep down that it's not going to work? And the same logic holds for these kids on panicking, or on being generally disinterested in the test and their score.

This disincentive can be more difficult to dismantle. As a parent, you can't reconstruct your child's peer group or ask its members to think of your child differently. What you can do is make sure that your child understands his capabilities. You can show your child that he can concentrate on tests, that he can perform well under stressful situations, and that you're going to help him get the tools he needs to succeed. You can help your child get a glimpse of himself as a successful test-taker, and you can help him remember that by always treating him like the successful test-taker you want him to be.

PERCEPTIONS OF CONTROL

The main reason we wrote this book was to assure parents and students that taking the SAT is a knowable, controllable experience. The perception we're trying to correct is a major disincentive to changing negative testing behavior. If a student believes the test is unknowable and uncontrollable, he has no incentive to *try* to know it and to *try* to control it. Why attempt the impossible?

When Amanda brought her past LSAT practice tests to show me, she fanned them out on the table and chanted her scores: 143, 147, 156, and 146. "See?" she exclaimed breezily, "There's no rhyme or reason for it. I'm all over the map and I have no idea why." She had no idea why because she didn't want to know why. It went against her view of the test to try to explain it or find reasons for the disparities in her score. She would rather confirm her belief that the LSAT was a terrible and confusing test, and one had better keep one's head down and barrel through it.

If, on the other hand, these tests are known, predictable quantities, and one could actually engineer one's way through them, well that left Amanda in quite a spot. She would have to take responsibility for her past SAT snafu and, more importantly, really buckle down to prepare for the LSAT. While that's awkward for Amanda in the short run, in the long run that's the answer she wants to hear. That is, after all, why she keeps returning to tutoring sessions and working on the test—she hopes that somehow, someday, she'll be able to get the test under control.

It hardly needs spelling out how to dispel this disincentive. The SAT is one of the most knowable, controllable tests around. It has to be. Yet, because it's such a radically different test from other tests that high school students take, it seems much more mysterious than it is.

Get information to your child. Let him know how the test works, what information is on it, and help your child see his progress as he studies. If he can see a little progress, he'll understand that more is possible.

TAKING RESPONSIBILITY (OR NOT)

Anxiety tends to remove responsibility from the anxious person. After all, if you have a panic attack, how can that be your fault? As these students are preparing to move from the world of kids to the world of adults, they are, in many cases, not ready to take full responsibility for all of their performances. For something as major as the SAT, being fully responsible for the score can be a very scary thing. It is a whole lot easier to say "I'm a bad test-taker" than it is to try to become a good test-taker.

Unfortunately, this disincentive is strengthened, rather than weakened, by most efforts to help students with anxiety. As the student receives more attention, the message that this problem is not her fault tends to grow in intensity. The thornier a problem with anxiety becomes, the more difficult it is to deal with, and the more legitimate it therefore seems. While some forms of anxiety do require professional psychological intervention and therefore should be treated as such, many kids allow themselves to indulge in anxious test-taking behavior at least partially as a way of ducking the ponderous responsibility that the SAT holds for them.

Keep in mind, stress is a grown-up emotion, one that kids watch their parents struggle with. I often ask kids how their parents deal with stress, and their answers are enlightening. "My mom gets really tense and grumpy, and snaps at us a lot." "My dad disappears for hours on end." Generally, the student doesn't relate healthy, successful methods for dealing with stress that he's learned from watching his parents. What kids have learned is that stress is everywhere and happens to everyone, and not even their parents can handle it. That's a pretty big disincentive for a 16- or 17-year-old to overcome. Why tackle a problem that even your parents can't solve? And how can that be your responsibility anyway?

This situation plays out in my office in a number of ways. The first indicator is often the level of involvement the student displays in the process: Mom makes the appointments, Mom delivers the kid, Mom answers all the questions that I direct to the child. The next step occurs when it's time to do homework or remember to bring materials. If a child consistently "forgets" to do her work or show up on time, the chances are good that she's experiencing a strong disincentive to take responsibility for her SAT experience. This is also fairly easy to detect at home, when a child seems to take no interest in preparing for the test or following through with the registration process.

Helping a child feel capable of taking responsibility over this process is half of the battle. Students need to feel not only that they can handle this test, but that they want to really take charge of this experience. Students should be involved in the decision making every step of the way, from when to take the test to how to prepare. Again, giving students a better understanding of the nature of the test and the testing process will help them feel more in control and better able to take responsibility. Finally, and perhaps most critically, students need to get the message that anxiety is normal and controllable, and that there are resources available to help them overcome it.

Removing disincentives to responsibility provides a bonus worth much more than a stellar SAT score: an empowered, self-reliant young adult who leaves for college able to confront obstacles with confidence born of experience. And that's what we want, right? We want our young people not only to succeed on this test, but to learn how to succeed on their own, on the many, many tests that life will present.

SELF-IMAGE

Remember what Amanda said? "I'm horrible at tests. I always freak out." At some point Amanda became invested in her testing personality, and she's sticking to it. To think otherwise would require a major paradigm shift for her, as well as the necessity of confronting some pretty uncomfortable possibilities—such as the possibility that had she learned to control her anxiety back in high school, she would have done much better on the SAT.

In our test-happy society, we tend to feel fairly intimate with our particular testing stratum. It's comforting to be a solid B+ student, and even more comforting to receive a commensurate SAT score. We'd like to believe these tests are fair tests of intelligence; we need to know that they mean something. After having lived the trauma of her SAT experience, Amanda needed to own it. Otherwise she'd have to prove herself wrong, and that's not just laborious but self-condemning. Besides, if she did fantastically on the SAT, how could she explain her B+ GPA?

By believing that she was only a fairly good SAT scorer who had issues with anxiety, Amanda also did not have to confront the highest levels of competition. She didn't have to send applications to the top schools that reject 90 percent of their applicants; she didn't have to face prolonged suspense followed by failure. She could go to a college she knew she'd be comfortable attending. She could force some of the ever-changing landscape of late high school to stay steady. It's one thing to leave home, of course, but quite another to jump into an arena more competitive than the one you're jumping from.

To overcome this disincentive, Amanda needed to be able to invest in a self-image as a good test-taker, and needed to be able to invest without risk. She needed positive testing experiences in situations free of consequences, and that comes with practice. By prepping her carefully for practice test situations and breaking down the results in a way in which she could see her progress and her successes, she began to slowly, risk-free, think of herself as a person who could perform well on tests. While positive talk is critical to helping someone change a testing self-image, providing proof is much more convincing.

FEAR

This last disincentive underlies all of the others. For the typical high school student, the SAT is actually a very difficult test. A major disincentive to changing a testing *modus operandi* significantly crippled by anxiety is the fear that even if you weren't scared, you still wouldn't know all those crazy words or be able to solve all those terrible math problems. To some extent, for almost every student, this fear is well founded.

Our teenagers are facing a terribly frightening world today and are expected to face it bravely. We don't spend a lot of time in our schools or homes discussing the fear that a car bomb or troubled teenager with a gun or suicide bomber or chemical weapon could, any second, obliterate us, wherever we are. Our teenagers deal with a tremendous amount of fear, largely in silence. Often, this fear works its way through these kids as stress, adding to their usual daily complexities.

I've worked with kids scared to death of the future, of this test, of failure, who didn't understand that it was these fears driving their various testing "dysfunctions." Many of these kids lack the ability to talk about the fear that drives them and so have little chance of overcoming it. Most of these kids have also been conditioned to believe that fear is not a socially appropriate emotion. Can you imagine a high school football star telling his math teacher he's frightened by a little test?

To root out this disincentive, I talk with the kids about their futures, their plans, and their possibilities. We discuss different outcomes and how we can respond to them. I use inclusive pronouns and try to let the kids know that they aren't facing this alone. At some point, many are able to pinpoint what exactly is worrying them—from not getting into the school their older siblings are attending, to having to retake the test, to disappointing their parents, to confirming their fears about their abilities. Once we discover the problem, we can work on the problem rather than succumb to the fear.

ON REMOVING DISINCENTIVES

If these are some of the disincentives that some high school students face, how can they be removed, or better yet, never put in place? It's actually not as daunting a task as it appears. The first method is one that this book visits and revisits throughout: give the student a taste of success. Let Amanda know what she's capable of, teach her how smart she is, show her how to succeed. If she knows she can be successful, really successful, then half of the disincentives will disappear automatically. She'll begin to see herself as capable and competitive, and begin to invest in that persona.

To accomplish this, Amanda needed one-on-one tutoring that focused on discovering her strengths and stripped away the encumbrances that discouraged her and prevented her from feeling personally successful. Other students find success in other ways. The important component here is that someone is taking the time to help that student feel successful and thus be successful on the test. Also, while success will be represented by a different score bracket for each tester, it can be reached by every student. And, if a student can consistently reach success in practice, his feelings about the test and himself will change. Only then will his testing behavior change.

Second, students who experience anxiety benefit from feeling that their burdens are shared with a parent or trusted adult, and sometimes a parent *and* a trusted adult. It's frightening to be a teenager about to take a test imbued with the anxiety of a nation, and feeling that someone is there to help navigate that course is invaluable. Don't tell your student, "Oh, I'm so sorry," and baby them. Instead say, "Well, that's OK. Now how are we going to solve that problem for next time?" For some students, all that is needed is a sense that the process is being shared, that it's a team effort to solve the problem. Parents can help plot out a study course or sit in on study sessions. Students can attend a class or a tutoring session to get some expert input. An appointment with a guidance counselor can help a student feel that someone is there to help him get ready for college and put together those fearsome applications. An older sibling can be available to answer questions.

The important commonality in the suggestions above is twofold: the human contact is one-on-one, and the person assisting is offering a shared responsibility in both the preparation and the outcome. When Amanda understood that I was there to help, and that I cared about her personally and how her test day went, she felt that she was not alone with her panic. She didn't need to push all responsibility for her poor performance on to her anxiety but could rely on me to help shoulder the burden. I have another student whose mother drives her to her tutoring appointment and sits in the lobby reading a book. Sure, she could head off to Starbucks, but she doesn't. While my student acts embarrassed and annoyed at this terribly motherly behavior, she knows she isn't alone in this project and she won't feel alone on the test.

Of course, the payoff for helping our young people find and use the tools they need to succeed on the SAT is that the very act of conquering the SAT teaches them the skills they need to succeed throughout the next stage of their lives. A student who has learned to control anxiety does not need to fear finals week at a prestigious university. A student who is self-motivated and self-confident will choose a major that matches his dreams, not his insecurities. A student who can overcome fear will be ready to face the social, emotional, *and* academic pressures of modern college life.

CHAPTER SEVEN

Learning Differences and Your Child

My student Joel was a nearly completely visual learner. I'm an auditory learner; I learn best by hearing and so, predictably, tend to instruct by talking. After a time working with Joel, I got the sense that he was merely "yessing" when I tried to instruct or correct him. I got a lot of the "un-huhs," "yeahs," and "sures." That's the clue that teachers, tutors, and parents get that their kids aren't really hearing whatever important knowledge they're trying to bestow. For Joel, a diagnostic test confirmed it: he was a quintessentially visual learner. My carefully crafted instruction was falling almost entirely on deaf ears. Now, Joel had never been given diagnostic testing for disabilities. There was no need. He had no diagnosable learning disability, just a difference in his learning style that was quite significant.

Every child is different in his skills and abilities. When the disparity between or among different abilities is significant enough, it can be officially labeled as a disability. It's helpful for students and their parents to think of such differences as *differences*, not as defects. We all have different tasks or processes at which we are less able than others. Becoming aware of them is of great benefit in that it can direct us to adjust our study habits or our behaviors to either remediate that relative weakness or to work around that difference.

We've discussed all sorts of underlying causes for underperformance, from anxiety to misinformation to debilitating family or peer dynamics. In this chapter, we'll approach one of the most controversial subjects surrounding the SAT: learning disabilities and the accommodations ETS makes for them. We'll discuss this issue from a tutoring perspective—partly because we're not clinical psychiatrists, and partly because the information and manifestations are somewhat different when it comes to the SAT. This chapter won't diagnose or treat your child's learning difference, but it should give you some insights about how to help your child perform his best on the SAT. In the case of the standardized test industry, learning differences are often either under-diagnosed or overdiagnosed, neither situation accruing to the ultimate benefit of the test-takers.

Many parents may be tempted to skip this chapter, relying on incomplete understandings or assumptions about learning differences and how they may or may not apply to their children. If you are seeing a pattern of underperformance on standardized tests, don't rule out the possibility that your child, however brilliantly he may be performing in other academic settings, may be struggling with the effects of a learning difference. For many parents, the SAT gives them the first clue that their child may have a different style or different struggle.

From visual processing disorders to executive functioning disorders to attention deficit disorder, the SAT has a certain ability to reveal those neuropsychological and physical differences that the people at your child's school might not have noticed. No other academic program or process is quite as unforgiving as this particular standardized test. In no other setting is such anonymity and rigidity enforced. A student who has coped successfully with a mild learning difference in the past doesn't realize how much he has relied on his teacher's visual cues, for example, or verbal explanations, or a classmate's extra set of notes. The SAT doesn't provide much wiggle room, however, and thereby often brings to light an otherwise unexplainable dip in a student's academic record.

For instance, as we noted earlier, many high school students, while not being actually functionally illiterate, read almost nothing throughout the four years of high school. These aren't kids who are getting by on SparkNotes in Shakespeare class to avoid the archaic poetic phrasing, but kids who literally don't read any of their assignments and still manage to rack up perfectly acceptable report cards. Getting through the SAT usually doesn't go very well for those students. Consider the students who tend to mix up numbers but have always been given partial credit on their math exams at school. The SAT doesn't give partial credit. And there are still other students whose attention-deficit tendencies have been tempered by short high school classes and pop quizzes. During the five hours of the extended-time SAT, those tendencies lunge forward.

Underperformance on the SAT certainly doesn't always indicate a disability or learning difference of some sort; indeed, the bulk of this book explores alternative explanations for underperformance. Clearly, there are disadvantages to blindly accusing insecure high school students of suffering from disorders merely because the SAT didn't go so well. I see parents pushing diagnoses on reluctant teenagers who feel humiliated by labels. I see parents transparently explaining a low score with a learning difference, sending the message to their child that his performance was so unacceptable as to be otherwise unexplainable. I also see teenagers diagnosed with imagined disabilities simply to secure the advantage of testing accommodations, and I wonder how many years that child will believe that he's not capable of success without dishonesty.

Wherever you and your child are, you cannot afford to ignore the issue of learning differences and testing accommodations. Your child may have a nontraditional learning difference that deserves attention, or nontraditional symptoms for a very traditional learning difference. You may be seeking accommodations for a child who does not want them or may not need them. Think about the issues in this chapter and discuss them with your child and your child's teacher to determine what is best for your child and your family.

ACCOMMODATIONS

College Board grants various testing accommodations for diagnosed learning disabilities, ADD/ADHD, specific psychological issues, and a host of physical and neurological issues from visual tracking to dysgraphia. The "Test Takers with Disabilities" section of the ETS website explains that test accommodations are individualized: no set of accommodations will be appropriate for all test-takers, and accommodations are granted in the style and to the degree needed by a particular student.[1]

All sorts of accommodations are offered and administered, from large-print test booklets or readers for the visually impaired, to wheel-chair access and specialized physical aids for the physically impaired, to extended breaks for diabetics. The most popular, most sought-after, and most valuable accommodation is by far extra time. ETS grants extra time testing for a range of supplicants, from those whose physical disabilities cause early-onset or debilitating exhaustion to those who can document any one of a number of learning differences. What makes extra time such a popular accommodation is that on a timed exam not just the disabled benefit from a lengthier testing period. While only visually impaired students would benefit from a Braille version of the test booklet, extra time favors nearly all test-takers, disabled or not.

There are two basic types of extra time accommodations. "Extended time" testing allows a student 50 percent extra time per section, so sections that are 25 minutes timed are now 37.5 minutes. (Students should naturally expect to get 37, not 38 minutes, as proctors are rarely that exacting.) Significantly, students may not move on to the next section even if they finish early. Happily, students taking the test with extended time accommodations do not have to take what used to be called the experimental section of the SAT, an unmarked and unscored extra section that ETS uses to vet new SAT questions. Three hours and forty-five minutes has now become an even five hours. With filling out forms and breaks, students can expect to be there from 8 AM to nearly 2 PM. For "double time" accommodations, students are given 50 minutes for each 25 minute section. Again, students taking the SAT under these conditions do not have to take the experimental section. Perhaps more significantly, students taking the test with double time take the test at their own school, and schools have the latitude to administer the test over the course of two days. This can be a huge coup, because if a student only has to take half of the test each day, she has a much better chance of sustaining the energy and concentration needed to perform optimally on the test.

For either test accommodation, students must fill out the requisite forms with College Board and have the same accommodations that they are applying for in place in their own schools. College Board understandably takes a dim view of students who discover they need extra time simply for standardized tests but have never needed it for academic tests in school. College Board now insists that students have accommodations in place in their high schools for four months prior to taking a College Board test with accommodations. Requisite documentation for accommodations usually involves psychoeducational testing done by a professional at the child's school or by an independent tester. Parents can expect independent testing to cost several hundred to several thousand dollars and involve two days of testing, and will find that the most highly regarded testers will have their schedules booked several months in advance.

How do extended or double time accommodations affect how you take the test? The great part about having extended time is that you should arguably have all the time you need to take the test. All of those reading passages that eat up so much testing time should not terrorize the student with extra time on his side. However, students need to recognize that although they have seemingly limitless time, they will not have limitless energy. Fatigue is the worst enemy of those students battling the test with extra time accommodations. For regular time students, the SAT is a perniciously long test. For extra time students, it can feel like a grueling death march. In most cases, getting the scores that they want involves answering the appropriate number of questions and purposefully skipping other ones in order to conserve energy.

Speaking of energy deprivation, students should "medicate" with appropriate snacks. As of the spring of 2005, students with extended time were not granted extra breaks, receiving the same five-minute break after the second section, one-minute break after the fourth section, and five-minute break after the sixth section. That's absurd. It is inordinately difficult to both go to the bathroom and consume some sort of snack in five minutes without being stressed out. Students should wear a watch and literally time their break so they know if they have three minutes left or one minute left, because it's very difficult to know how much time has passed. You don't want to return late to your room or be too anxious about doing so, nor do you want to not take advantage of your full break. For snacks, students should bring high energy snacks that they can consume quickly. One student shared with me her perfect snack solution: foil-topped single-servings of applesauce—you can pull off the lid and suck down the applesauce in seconds, efficiently ingesting about a hundred calories.

College Board has stated that it will continue to revisit the issue of appropriate breaks for both extended time and regular students. As of now, it stands by its earlier study of fatigue's effects on SAT scores, cheerfully declaring that there are none. Common sense and experience, of course, disagree. Does *your* teenage child have a five-hour attention span for academic work? If you are considering trying to get extra time for your child, it's important to know not just how to get it, but how it may affect your child and your child's testing experience.

DIAGNOSIS SHOPPING

When College Board bowed to a pending lawsuit over its flagging of scores on exams taken under nonstandard conditions, it only increased the controversy and claims of foul play. In the past, students who used any accommodation, whether extra time or a special computer or a sign language interpreter, had an asterisk placed after their numerical SAT score to inform colleges that their test had been taken in a different way than others. While some appreciated the idea that colleges could make a more informed decision as to their ability to serve that potential student, others bemoaned the stigma and assumed that those coveted admissions letters would be that much harder to snare because of that damning asterisk. Now that the asterisk has been banished, even the disability community isn't sure that the situation is better.

College Board, assuming that the unflagging of scores would act as an invitation to mildly disabled or even fully able students to vie for extra time, promptly began measures to tighten its application process for accommodations. Requests for accommodations have actually declined since that time, but some interesting demographic shifts have been noted. Neuropsychologists-for-hire are thriving in this new environment, and certain geographic regions and even particular private high schools are rumored to be gobbling up the lion's share of the coveted, nonstigmatized, extra-time accommodations. Something somewhere is askew.[2]

Amid the controversy, College Board steadfastly claims that any gaming of the system is negligible.[3] Students who get accommodations deserve accommodations, they declare, and any inequity that may result is surely no greater than the existing educational and socioeconomic inequities we've come to accept. The statistics, however, are enough to give a nonbiased observer pause if not alarm.

In order to gain special accommodations on any College Board exam, a student must undergo a thorough battery of psychological tests, usually over the course of several days. The most productive, and therefore prized, psychoeducational consultants often maintain a waiting list of clients seeking diagnoses, especially in the months leading up to a major SAT exam. Increasingly, consultants are reporting that their clientele is shifting toward junior- and senior-level high school students, well past the age that a useful diagnosis can and should be made.

While College Board makes special accommodation information readily available on its website, the process of securing those accommodations is more than just expensive and time consuming. It can be intricate, confusing, and some claim, arbitrary. These factors together are enough to ensure that the bulk of economically disadvantaged inner-city students will have little opportunity to secure accommodations. These factors also ensure that wealthy, savvy, and motivated parents will more often win the precious extra time for their children's SAT.

And, to the limited extent that we can obtain demographic information on this issue, that looks exactly like what is happening. As an aftereffect, the year after the asterisk for special circumstances was dropped, test scores on exams taken under standard conditions remained stagnant while those on exams taken under nonstandard conditions jumped. Indeed, in Washington, DC, unlike in the United States as a whole, special testers have maintained a significant score advantage over regular testers for some years, a statistic that strains the credibility of the argument that accommodations simply level the playing field. A graph of this trend eerily echoes the widening gap in the Washington area and elsewhere in the country between the haves and the have-nots.[4]

Adding to the advantages for the economically privileged is another of College Board's requirements for special accommodations. Remember, whatever accommodations a student requests for taking the SAT, his school must already be using them for his academic tests at least four months before the SAT. Cash-strapped public schools have much more difficulty arranging for many students to take double time biology quizzes proctored in afterschool hours. On the other hand, ambitious private schools have a greater ability to arrange class schedules to accommodate double time testing; they have plenty of specialized staff members available to ensure that any student who can get a diagnosis can secure the accommodations needed.

Talk to any educational consultant operating in today's college admissions market and you'll hear the same story. Unquestionably, the system is being abused. It may be that only a fraction of the students are obtaining accommodations inappropriately, or it may be more. Unquestionably, more parents are taking advantage of extra time accommodations for students who up until then had shown little need for extra help. The parents with the advantage are those who have money for expensive and liberal psychoeducational testers—testers rumored to be willing to give anyone with enough money a disability diagnosis—as well as money to retain attorneys to fight negative rulings from ETS. For these parents, this is one more smart way to ensure that their child snares a slot in that top-choice school.

For many, the issue comes down to what it means to justify extra time accommodations. I hear parents say that their son or their daughter would really benefit from extra time on the test. I hear professionals explain that if you take a practice test with 50 percent more time and see a significant difference in scores, then you would benefit from additional minutes. And College Board reports that for the low-scoring students they studied, extra time has little to no benefit and therefore does not constitute an unfair advantage.

The data suggests that the trend is racing toward more higher-scoring students taking the test with extra time, while lower-scoring students are applying for accommodations in fewer—or at least not increasing—numbers. SAT time constraints, however, are only restrictive to those students who have the intellectual ability but not the speed to work through more questions. On a timed test, a student capable of answering most of the questions will improve with more time to spend on each question. For those students whose test scores are limited by lack of knowledge and ability, arguably the extra time won't always make that much of a difference, as College Board maintains. The old assumptions and information regarding extra time testing simply don't apply nearly as well to the new generation of ambitious, privileged, and overaccommodated test-takers.

What this means for your child is that securing extra time for testing is hotly debated. If your child has already been diagnosed with a learning difference that may justify testing accommodations, lose no time in submitting the required paperwork to ETS—you may have a fight in front of you. With regulations tightening and accusations flying, you'll need extra time yourself to make sure your child gets the accommodations he needs.

WARNING SIGNS

Just how do you know if your child should be tested for a learning difference? Without obvious symptoms, it can be difficult to know if your child has a reading problem, a processing problem, an anxiety problem, or an attitude problem. Often, it's a combination of two or more of those. There are a few signs that every parent should watch for, even in high-scoring kids. You want to give your child the best chance you can for the SAT, for higher education, and for a successful career.

First, keep in mind that learning differences don't automatically make students below average or less intelligent. Many of the kids I tutor score in the top percentiles, accommodations or no accommodations. Just because your child does well in school doesn't mean she's not masking a learning difference that could improve with diagnosis and treatment.

Look for the anomalies in performance. Is your daughter's homework stellar but test scores low? Is her GPA high but standardized test scores tanking? Does she do great on tests but torpedo her grades by failing to hand in completed assignments? Is she excelling in some academic classes and failing others? Kids with learning differences often depend on cues, crutches, extra credit, and extra time to get their work done, and when those variables change, often their scores do as well.

What about anxiety? Does your son struggle to control his panic on tests? Does he sweat assignments that his classmates do easily? Does it seem to take more determination and more emotional energy to get through quizzes and projects? He may be working through more than just the normal load of homework; he may be fighting a learning or anxiety disorder as well.

Do you suspect your child of experimenting with smoking? Many kids who struggle with attention deficit difficulties are, usually unknowingly, self-medicating with nicotine. If you think your child smokes, if you have a history of ADD/ADHD in your family, if your child has a high level of distractibility—these symptoms point to ADD/ADHD and may be worth further investigation.

Does your child hate reading? Have her read aloud to you, and pay attention to the fluidity and ease with which she works through the text. Jot down some notes, and make an appointment with your school's reading specialist. It doesn't hurt to do a little preliminary detective work. If nothing else, it can put your mind at ease.

Look for signs of depression and other mood disorders. Depression, bipolar disorder, obsessive-compulsive disorder—all of these are surprisingly common among high school students. Not only should these be treated while your child is young, but they can affect school and test performance as well.

Not all underperformance problems on the SAT are a result of learning differences, physical disorders, or emotional and mental problems. Not all anxiety is clinical or debilitating, and not all performance glitches need to be treated by a psychiatrist. If you're serious about helping your child remove all his personal obstacles to success, however, you've got to make sure you've been as thorough as you can be. There are many undiagnosed children taking the SAT who could really use the help.

ADD/ADHD

Not only are there many different types of learning differences, but the way a learning difference manifests itself differs from child to child. The example below is not a diagnosis or a treatment plan for ADD/ADHD; it is an example of one way that a disorder combined with other factors to cause underperformance on the SAT for one of my students. As with all the student examples in this book, the causes for each student's underperformance are complex and unique and the cure for underperformance must therefore be individualized. This example illustrates how learning differences and disorders can interplay with anxiety, family dynamics, and the SAT.

Emma
Emma had what some would call a double disadvantage: ADHD and prominent, successful parents. She showed classic signs of teenage shutdown: feigning total inability in order to avoid struggling to

achieve at a level that could never be high enough anyway. She ex-
plained to me that she hadn't read a book in years, and that despite
her complete lack of effort, she was managing to pass her classes with
low C's and D's. Needless to say, assigning Emma SAT homework
was futile.

Looking over Emma's PSAT report, I saw a familiar pattern.
With only half as many sections as the SAT, the PSAT sometimes al-
lows for a clearer look at a student's testing habits, divorced from the
endurance and fatigue effects of the longer exam. Emma's PSATs
told a clear story. Each section began with a few correct answers, then
proceeded to a mix of correct, incorrect, and skipped questions, and
then the section's last third went completely unanswered. Seeing this
pattern continue over five sections, I could almost feel her discourage-
ment and panic as she lost the ability to focus and control her mind
while the clock ticked on. Where a new section began, she would start
anew, answering the first few correctly and then hitting the more be-
wildering questions just as her attention began to wander.

Unfortunately, the raw score didn't provide as much texture for
Emma's discouraged parents. They saw a score well below average
and a daughter who seemed to not care at all. In this case, fixing the
problem would entail much more than having Emma bank a few vo-
cabulary words and memorize a math trick or two. Emma had to
battle the very way that she thought and performed academically.

Classically, ADD/ADHD is the inability to inhibit or control impulsiv-
ity. In other words, sudden impulses to a person with ADD/ADHD become mandates. While a "typical" person taking a test might get
frustrated on a question or reading passage and want to throw down his
pencil and forget it, he probably will just hang onto that pencil and give
the annoying question one more try. Someone with ADD/ADHD,
however, will be more likely to skip the question, or may actually throw
that pencil on the floor and walk away from the test.

To compound the problem, questions on the SAT often require
four to five steps to reach the correct answer. A student can complete
three steps correctly, honestly think he's done with the question, move
on too quickly under the pressure of time, and miss the problem entirely. Students with ADD/ADHD are much more likely to fall into
this trap. I've seen students work through a math section, do half to

two-thirds of each problem correctly, and then get incorrect answers for almost the entire section.

Besides the obvious problem of underperforming on these sections, the abysmal scores these students receive cause increased pressure to perform and decreased confidence in ability. Now the students are working harder, faster, and carrying more stress, which in turn multiplies the problem. Students can end up feeling utterly paralyzed by a math section filled with problems they actually know how to do.

Take a look at this problem:

If the average (arithmetic mean) of 13, 7, 6, 14, and x is equal to x, what is the value of 2x?

Many students will have no problem computing the math elegantly, arriving at a correct value for x, in the following way. First, they'll find the sum of the terms:

$$13 + 7 + 6 + 14 + x = 40 + x$$

They will then divide $40 + x$ by 5, and set that equal to x.

$$\frac{40 + x}{5} = x$$
$$40 + x = 5x$$
$$40 = 4x$$
$$10 = x$$

They'll get this answer wrong. The question, at its terminus, requests the definition for 2x, an additional and incredibly simple step, but one that most students won't naturally remember. The answer to this problem isn't 10, although you can bet that the SAT will provide that as an answer choice. Remember, ETS needs that bell curve and straightforward algebraic questions won't always produce that. At a certain point, this math question, so similar to dozens or hundreds that the students have calculated in the past, will trigger a habitual process or response. As students fall into the routine of solving for x, a very comfortable process, they will feel a familiar sense of victory and completion upon finding x, and fill in the bubble for 10 as their answer. ETS counts on that.

Here, the students who miss this question do so not because they don't know how to find 2x, but because they don't remember what it is they are solving for. And the students who are most likely to make this error will be those who struggle with ADD/ADHD, because once they've solved for x, their minds have jumped ahead to the next question.

What can be done? I counsel students to start forming new habits, very specific ones. As they read through each math question, they should circle exactly what it is the question is asking, whether it be x or 2x or the average of b and c. Then, when solving the problem, they should check their answer against the question's demanded response. Finally, before filling in the answer choice, they should reread the question and make sure they didn't overlook a critical piece of information buried somewhere in the text. Sure, it's laborious work, but that's what the extra time is for.

Emma's Strategy

Even after Emma and I discussed and practiced the methods and tricks she'd need to compensate for both her learning difference and the psychological manipulation of the SAT, she still wasn't ready to work through a full-length test. Just knowing what to do isn't enough for anybody; for the student with ADD/ADHD it's often nowhere near sufficient. Emma was smart enough to work most of the problems on the SAT, but her learning difference wasn't giving her the chance to show that.

Each time Emma came into my office, I'd spend ten minutes going over our plan, emphasizing her need to reread questions, to skip broadly, and to not waste her energy on the final 20 percent of questions in each section. We'd talk about specific strategies for the math section, for example, and then I'd hand her a timer and a 30-minute math SAT section, and leave the room. Thirty minutes later, she'd hand me a picture-perfect score sheet. The next week we'd do critical reading, and the next, writing. In carefully orchestrated spurts, Emma rocked the test.

For Emma, it was something of a revelation that she was actually good at the SAT. Instead of feeling a jumble of frustration and stress and seeing a rock-bottom score at the end of it, she was having positive and successful experiences with the SAT. For the first time, she could separate her intelligence and ability from the welter of pressures and failures that the SAT had been thus far in her life. For Emma, this was invaluable.

For Emma's parents, it was the validation they'd been looking for that their daughter was capable of doing well. When Emma was able to show them her above-average scores, she altered the negative SAT dynamic they'd been experiencing. It wasn't that she couldn't pretend to be utterly incapable anymore; it was that she didn't have to. Her successes multiplied as she proved to her parents what she could do when it was on her own terms.

Don't forget that one of the symptoms of ADD/ADHD is that kids have a hard time sticking with things—SAT preparation and performance included. There are quite a few methods you can use to help your child make the most of his SAT preparation time and develop good habits that will help him endure the marathon of the SAT. Most important to remember is that productive and successful preparation will give your child the confidence and positive habits that will carry him through on test day.

People tend to remember the beginnings and ends of things much more than the middles. Think of the movies you've seen recently, or books you've read. For someone with ADD/ADHD, this trend is intensified. In many cases, therefore, it's sensible to break things up, creating more beginnings and more ends. Twenty minutes of math, then 5 minutes of vocabulary, then another 20 minutes of math, for instance. It's like working out at the gym: if you have only 30 minutes, you'll make the most of that time. With an hour and a half to kill, you'll probably kill half of it goofing around. If you fool your brain into thinking that there are more beginnings and endings, more intervals, you'll get more done, more efficiently.

With typical test-takers in my office, I see them settle in to a practice test, starting out slower and more jumpy, and then hitting their stride about 20 minutes in. With students who have ADD/ADHD, the pattern is different. These kids are highly motivated and start out strong, but peter out in about 20 minutes. For them, the longer the test, the lower the score, guaranteed.

Just as Emma learned, working in snatches and spurts often captures the best energy of an ADD/ADHD student. After all, we're looking to exploit the strengths of each test-taker, and starting strong is definitely a worthwhile strength. Try having your child study vocabulary in five-minute bursts. Set a timer for 15 minutes, and tell your son to walk away from the math book when the buzzer goes off. When your child concentrates on one section at a time, he can be successful at studying and at mastering the material he's studying. Students with ADD/ADHD are often highly intelligent and bring an unrivaled positive intensity to their bouts of attention.

If you give your son two hours and a stack of materials, on the other hand, he'll most likely not only fail at learning the material, but he will feel frustrated at his inability to finish the assignment. He'll then feel worse about working on the material, and feel worse about himself. For this type of scenario, forcing a practice test a day can be the most detrimental thing you can do, despite your best intentions.

People tend to feel good about themselves to the degree that they are successful completing projects or assignments. Your child must feel successful at each step along the way before she can go on to the next step and be successful. Try to set your children up for success by having them develop habits that lead them to success, rather than flogging them daily to get them to do things that are unpleasant for them to do. When you get your children to do five minutes of vocabulary a day and then congratulate them, they associate positive feelings of success and approbation with vocabulary practice. They feel good about what they have done rather than discouraged about what they haven't done. They'll be more likely to study tomorrow, and more likely to feel confident on the day of the test.

Emma's Endurance

Unfortunately, even with accommodations, including multiple-day testing, Emma still couldn't take the test in the 30-minute spurts we initially practiced. It's ironic that the test-takers who are the most disadvantaged by the gargantuan length of the SAT have to take a test that is 50 to100 percent longer. For many students with ADD/ ADHD, the extra time is just that much more rope to hang themselves with, as the minutes and hours compound the frustration and panic. Emma was no different. Proving that she could succeed for 30 minutes was nowhere near enough to ensure that she'd perform optimally for 5 hours.

Emma worked on endurance. She learned how to block out the last part of a section and move on to the next one. She tried to tame her focus and discipline her timing. As much progress as she made, however, she knew that for her, test day would take all the energy and focus that she could bring. There are, actually, lots of strategies to help someone with ADD/ADHD do their best on a lengthy standardized test. As with any learning or performance difference, educational professionals can help develop individualized plans for maximizing a student's strengths. My job was to make sure that she knew that her best was going to be good enough. With that knowledge and her practiced endurance, Emma was ready to give it her all on the day of the test. Perhaps the SAT would never capture her strengths and abilities the way we'd like, but Emma and I made sure it wouldn't hold her back from fulfilling her academic goals.

***

Every child learns and performs differently, and every learning difference, disorder, and disability appears differently each time. I emphasize to my students that no one is a born test-taker. For those people who have superlative test-taking abilities, the years after high school must look pretty bleak. For the rest of us, we learn to tailor our skills to the standardized task at hand.

This goes for students with learning differences as well. I tell my students that they aren't sunk just because they've been tagged with executive functioning disorder, or dyslexia, or visual processing disorder, or ADD/ADHD. Like everyone else, they've got to find their strengths and bend them toward the SAT. Like everyone else, that process is likely to uncover some surprising abilities and talents.

For my students who work through learning differences and accommodations, the tasks are the same: learn to understand the test, your own patterns and motivations, and conquer your fears and your anxiety. The SAT is about what you can do, not what you can't. And for those students who have conquered not only the SAT but a learning difference or disability as well, the celebrations are that much sweeter. And the lessons they learn about overcoming limitations and personal obstacles will carry them much farther than an SAT score ever could.

IV

Uncovering the Causes
of Underperformance

CHAPTER EIGHT

Communication

I tutored a really nice boy named Tyson, whose spring break fell right before the SAT. Like most high school juniors, he really wanted to go to his school party—Beach Week at Duck Beach—that week. Who wouldn't? It's a week of rampant partying with no parental restraints right smack in the middle of the most stressful part of high school. Tyson's dad, however, was worried about how that week would affect his performance on the SAT. Tyson and I talked about it, and agreed that he would come home from Beach Week by Thursday afternoon at the latest. That would give him two good nights of sleep before the test, as well as time to come see me on Friday just before the test on Saturday. He'd be thoroughly rested and steady before the test.

Friday rolled around the week of the SAT, and Tyson showed up as planned. He was a bit more tan, and bit a more subdued. "Everything OK? I hope none of your wacky friends got arrested at Beach Week!" I joked. He reported that everything was fine and he was ready for the test. He seemed on edge and distracted, however, as I gave him some final pointers and sent him off to take the test.

He tanked the test. Royally. And I was clueless as to why.

Well, later, Tyson's dad stepped in to explain. Tyson was a really nice guy, but in the first thrill of Beach Week, he'd made a few poor judgments, and had himself, in fact, been arrested. After a night in a jail cell, an arraignment, a hearing, and a week full of mortification, he had just made it back in time for our tutoring appointment and the *test the next day. And, after my oh-so-clever joke, the poor guy felt unable to tell me the truth and let me help him deal with how his horrible week might affect his SAT performance. Instead, he lied, was too distracted to be able to pay any attention to my advice, and then dive-bombed on the test. He, understandably, was completely unable to pull himself together without help.*

And I'd made it so he couldn't ask for the help he needed to succeed!

The depressing thing about this story is that, taking the long view, getting arrested at Beach Week really isn't that big a deal. For Tyson, it probably scared him into a lifetime of sobriety and driving just under the speed limit. But getting arrested and then tanking the SAT in the same week—well, that can really set a kid to wondering whether he's going to make it out there as an adult.

In addition, sometimes we adopt a "one strike you're out" mentality with kids that can be far harsher than we intend. Just as attending the wrong party shouldn't make a kid feel labeled for life, so flubbing one SAT shouldn't make a kid a bad test-taker. What often happens is the "good kids" end up being the lucky ones who aren't caught in their youthful indiscretions on their bad days, while the "bad kids" are just plain unlucky. By sending students the message that one mistake will ruin their lives, we're exponentially increasing the pressure they feel to perform on all the tests life gives them.

The teenagers themselves understand this, and they also understand what happens if you get caught and labeled a "bad kid." What this young man needed was validation that he had made a bad choice but was not a bad person. Absolutely, there should be consequences, but condemnation by his SAT tutor should not be one of them. Tyson needed the support and encouragement to allow him to understand that high school years are turbulent, and that mistakes can be atoned for. At the very least, that understanding would have allowed him to more readily absorb a misstep on the SAT and move forward with the confidence to get the rest of the exam correct.

So how do you make it safe for your children to tell you the truth? Let's explore that through a few basic communication tools: expressing interest, asking questions, being patient, and listening. Sound familiar? None of us are as good at talking to our children as we could be, and it can make all the difference in the world. And I'm not just referring to the SAT.

COMMUNICATION TOOL 1:
EXPRESS INTEREST IN THEIR INTERESTS

One of the most basic tools for establishing a rapport is to show genuine enthusiasm for the other person and the things that are important to her. This seems so obvious that it's tempting to just sweep it aside, but it's shocking how well it works. It's probably safe to say that my hobbies and interests rarely, if ever, intersect with those of my students. Through the years, however, I have come to appreciate and learn about all sorts of things from my students who are into drama, hockey, jumping horses, murder mysteries, Internet communities, and overwhelmingly profane music.

I have students whose tastes are utterly not mine, just as you may have kids who listen to music or enjoy activities that seem to you foolish or a complete waste of time. Even if you see the hours spent playing video games as wholly devoid of value, you can show interest in your son's hobby and enthusiasm for his video successes. When he sees you respect how he chooses to spend his free time, he'll be more likely to listen to you about the SAT, among other things.

Whenever I meet a new student in the fall, I start out by asking, "So what have you been doing with your summer?" Invariably, the answer tells me what is important to this person I'm seeking to get to know. And my response to the information I'm given is always, "Wow, that's great! I don't know anything about that. What's it all about?" And then, suddenly, the student likes me.

Okay, so the students don't really like *me*—they like the way they feel when they talk to me. They like feeling interesting and worthwhile. They like that I'm interested in their lives. It's like the often-heard suggestion to treat every person you meet as if she has a sticker on her forehead that says "make me feel important."

This is pretty easy, because I really am fascinated by what jazzes them. (Granted, no one to date has told me "Hey, I'm out drowning puppies"—it's usually something pretty cool.) One summer, however, a student named Melanie responded only with "Oh, I've been working." My follow-up question of "Where?" was met by "Couple of internships."

Rather cryptic. Here in the Washington, DC, area, internships are typically fairly exciting and certainly not something to hide. Melanie clearly felt reluctant to say where she had been working.

It is really important for people to be able to tell the truth. The problem is we don't regularly incentivize our children to do so. We ask for the truth and when told explode with "YOU DID WHAT?!" That doesn't exactly condition children to be candid in the future. When students confess to me that they didn't do their homework for whatever reason, I always say, "Well, thanks for telling me the truth. Is there anything we can do to help you get it done or was this just an unavoidable problem this week?" Then, we find a solution—or at least they are gently reminded that I really do want them to do well, and I think it's important for them to get this work done so that they can. To help steer behaviors in a helpful direction, it's important for me to talk to students in a way that actually encourages them to choose those behaviors.

Part of the way we express interest in people is to validate whatever it is that they are telling us. When I'm at my best, the first words that I respond with are something like, "Thank you for telling me," or "What an interesting idea," or "That's terrific." Validating is so critical because the most valuable skill that I can offer students or parents is diagnosis: Any effective remedy has to be based on a clear understanding of the problem. Understanding is difficult when you don't have the right information. Any good physician will tell you that it's the patients themselves who are the best sources of information, better than any test that can be run on expensive diagnostic machines. This means that getting the patients to tell you what is going on is vitally important. In other words, bedside manner matters.

Parents care about their children and want the best for them, but there can be long-term goals and short-term pressures that seem in conflict. Validating is the key to resolving such conflicts. If I don't validate first, I may be so concerned with getting to the solution of the immediate issue or in having my point heard that I fail to consider the long-term ramifications on my relationship with my child. The typical pattern I see is this: Your teen is caught or confesses to doing something that might be deemed to be at best ill-advised. As a parent, you have two interests: one, correcting that behavior, and two, understanding the reasons behind it. And remember, your child is the only one who can really shed light on the latter. Too often parents immediately begin on their first goal, correcting the behavior, and in their zeal ensure that their second goal, learning what caused that behavior, will never be met. Granted, it's hard to validate first when you are upset or angry or the behavior involves things that you feel "really matter." Consider, however, how hard it is to discover why your child was behaving so poorly once you've shut the door to communication. In my experience, it's really worth developing the habit of validating first.

Let's be clear, however. Validating does not mean that you have to agree with the opinion or behavior being discussed. "Mom, I smoked marijuana last night," or "Dad, I parked the car on the neighbor's lawn," does not have to be met with a cheerful, "Gee, honey, that's great!" If my son ever sets the couch on fire, such an action might understandably be met with, "What were you thinking?!" But, is that really a question, or is it angry criticism? Really, it's both. I have a legitimate interest in understanding and in correcting his behavior. My question-criticism won't do that. He'll only hear the criticism and I won't get an explanation; I'll get a defense. So, I might instead use validation to separate them. "Son, I really am glad you told me that the couch is on fire. Could you please tell me what was the reason you set fire to the furniture? I really am curious." Once I've gotten the information and better understand my son's thinking and, perhaps, how better to prevent future fires, I will, ideally, patiently reiterate our family rule against setting fire to the family furniture. By developing the habit of expressing appreciation, thanks, or interest in your children's thoughts, pleasant and unpleasant, you lubricate the gears of communication so that your children will actually talk to you and not just tell you what you want to hear.

So, 15 minutes later, I asked Melanie more directly to tell me about her internships. She had worked two internships with two top political figures. They were really, really cool internships—if your political affiliation heads in that direction. Her politics, at least those of the leaders she worked for, are distinctly not mine. But that's my problem. "Wow!" I said. "That must be really cool." Because it was, for her.

She exhaled. It was OK. She attends a school and lives in a town where her opinions are decidedly in the minority. And that's hard. Melanie is delightful but deferential. She is not combative in the least. So one can imagine that, in the past, she had been attacked and condemned for her beliefs, and that she had little ability to defend herself.

Naturally, she was inclined to keep her internship information to herself. Even so, I really was pleased for her. It sounded like a terrific experience. And because she felt I was genuinely pleased for her, she trusted me. She let her guard down. She could tell me the truth. And her ability to remain unguarded with me became important as we worked together on her SAT skills. When she didn't understand a question, it was safe for her to say "I don't know." It was safe for her to listen to me and to learn from me.

Make it safe to tell the truth—don't make the consequences too hard or too final. If you do, you are unlikely to get the truth, the whole truth, and nothing but the truth. Then, you will also be effectively left out of the loop and excluded from being part of the solution.

COMMUNICATION TOOL 2: ASK QUESTIONS

This was my big blunder with Tyson. Why didn't I just ask him how Beach Week went? Instead, I assumed that I knew what had happened and then made a joke. I've seen this happen over and over again, and when it does, communication stops.

It's so easy to believe that, as adults, we know more than our children, especially about their lives. To be honest, the SAT is really part of their lives, not ours. You can do all the research you want on ETS and extended time and math tricks, but the SAT is an experience for your child, not for you. Ask questions. Find out what your child thinks and how your child feels.

The first benefit of asking our children questions is that they immediately respect us, and immediately feel better about themselves and more capable. They know stuff, and you know it. They'll feel more in control of the situation, and they'll be more likely to take responsibility for their test preparation, among other things. Asking your children questions communicates that they are in charge and you trust them.

The second benefit of asking our children questions is that we really can get actual information from them. We find out what is going on at school, who got a perfect score and how, who is freaking out about the test, who thinks smoking a joint or using a friend's Ritalin prescription before the test is a good idea (which it isn't), and what scares our kids about this test. We learn why your daughter thinks she keeps running out of time on the math section, or why your son prefers to use a calculator. We're not steering blind anymore: we've got some insight on where the problems lie.

And when we ask our children questions, they'll be more likely to ask us questions. When kids know we're interested in them, they're a lot more open to hearing what we have to say. Of course, we'd all love it if our children cherished our spontaneous lectures on various topics, but wouldn't it be nice if our kids could ask us about the very things that worry them? Wouldn't you like to know what those things are?

COMMUNICATION TOOL 3: BE PATIENT

Our kids really do need to feel that it's safe to tell the truth—not just about what they've done but about how they feel. For kids (and adults, for that matter), so much of their seemingly irrational behavior is really an attempt to communicate something that they don't feel they can say straight out. Think of a two-year-old child screaming her head off in the grocery store after a full afternoon of errands. She isn't saying that she wants to embarrass her parent, or stress out the other shoppers, or create a terrible scene. She's expressing her exhaustion and need for a little attention, or food, or quiet time at home. She doesn't know a better communication strategy.

Teenagers are the same way; they need help expressing their feelings and telling the truth. Teenagers especially need to feel that whatever they say will be accepted and respected, no matter how horrifying it may be to the parent. This doesn't happen overnight. This takes patience.

One of the important things to remember is that teenagers, for all their reputation for chattiness, aren't always ready to talk. I know one mother of teenagers who stays up much later than she'd like in order to talk to her children when they come home from dates and parties. By consistently being awake, patient, and ready to nosh and dish, she earned the trust of her children and heard the things they weren't able to say over the breakfast table. I know a grandmother who very patiently chats about dolls and ponies on the phone with her eight-year-old granddaughter every day, in order to ensure that when that granddaughter becomes a teenager, she'll confide in her grandmother. In the fast-paced lives that so many of us have created for ourselves, this is so rarely the case. Studies of the benefits of families spending dinner together are measuring in large part the benefits of parents' unhurried time with children where conversations can take place at their own pace without having to be initiated and finished in the ten minutes that can be squeezed in between the end of soccer practice and the 5 PM Spanish tutor.

Helping your child feel safe to talk to you takes time. You'll find, however, that as you work to make this happen, much of the negative communication that may have impeded your relationship in the past will naturally fall away. When your child can tell you how he feels, your child will listen to your concerns as well.

COMMUNICATION TOOL 4: LISTEN TO THEM

I'm not kidding. Listen to what your kid is saying and try to figure out what he really means. Remember that no matter how good your relationship with your son may be, there's a good chance he doesn't feel able to fully tell you how he feels.

In today's world it's not okay to have fear. Especially for teenagers, it's not okay to say "I'm afraid." Worried about terrorists bombing your mom's downtown office building? C'mon, what are the odds? Concerned about that angry kid in a trench coat bringing guns to school? Yeah right, what is this, Columbine? Fearful that you'll bomb the SAT? Get a grip. It's just not okay for people to feel afraid in our society. Anxious or stressed is okay—in fact, being stressed has become quite the fashion.

This creates a situation in which people begin to understand that it's not appropriate to articulate directly what they're actually feeling or thinking. I hear: "I'm stressed out about taking this test because I want to do well enough to go to college." What I understand is quite different: "Really, I'm afraid that if I don't do well on this test people will think I'm not good enough, or smart enough. My parents will be mad and think I'm stupid. I won't be able to go to college and no one will like me." Who could say that in just those words?

When a teenager explains that he's stressed about the SAT, people can nod and say comforting things. "Oh, you'll be fine. I was stressed, too, when I took that test." Should the teenager decide to be honest about his feelings, he makes himself emotionally naked. People wouldn't know how to respond. Instead of talking around the problem, they would have to face it.

Chances are your child won't immediately be able to tell you he feels afraid. Address the issue anyway. Listen to how he feels, or how he may feel, when he states that he feels stressed. Thank him for telling you. Ask follow-up questions: "I am glad you told me. What are you most concerned about?" Resist the temptation to immediately offer a solution. Listen for cues that show that he can't verbalize how he really feels. Listen for his real concerns.

What's interesting is that, ultimately, we want our children to be successful on this test. More importantly, we want them to come out whole with their family relations and sense of self intact. I see parents berating their kids in ways they thought they would never do. If you call these parents on that behavior, they say in so many words that the SAT is really important and that they are therefore justified in losing their tempers with their kids. The message the kids receive is that what really matters is the score—not their relationship, not them. When it comes down to the heart of it, the child understands: "you're yelling at me because you care more about my getting into Cornell than you care about me." Parents, on the other hand, reply that all they care about is their child's success.

The result? Parents are frustrated and furious, continually losing their tempers and complaining to each other about their children's unwillingness to do what is best for them. Kids are frustrated and discouraged, believing their moms and dads are sure they're going to bomb this test. It's a shame, because usually the only thing wrong with this situation is communication. Everyone here wants the same thing, and everyone wants to help. Unfortunately, no one is helping.

Turning this around is really shamefully easy. What I've observed is that people are usually so concerned with making sure that their message is heard that they cannot listen fully to others. What's more, in their urgency to be understood, they neglect framing their comments in a way that would make them palatable to others. In my opinion, this is often the only communication problem for the kids and parents.

While this may be the only problem for many families, it's a deadly problem. Kids are shutting down while parents hit the roof. Kids aren't getting the support they need to perform up to their abilities while parents are setting the stage for worse and worse relationships with their children as the college years loom ahead. Our children find it nearly impossible to be successful when they believe that we don't believe in them.

Be the first one to step down. Let go of your need to communicate your message for a while. A week, maybe even two or three. The best-selling author Stephen Covey frames it as "seek first to understand, then to be understood."[1] Dedicate yourself to understanding what your child is saying, without trying to respond, disagree, overrule, or suggest. Express interest. Ask questions. Be patient. Listen. Give it some time. Remember, you have more communication skills at your disposal than your child does. Give him a head start.

When you do start to broadcast your message again, remember what you've learned about your child. Present your concerns and suggestions in a way that communicates this knowledge and confidence in his judgment.

"I admire the way you've worked on that tricky math concept—you've been really dedicated over the past week. Have you thought about asking your math teacher?"

"I know you love auto shows and that there will be one in town the weekend of the SAT. Do you think it would be a good idea to get tickets for Sunday instead of Friday so you know you'll be your best for the SAT?"

"It's really great that you care so much about doing your best. I can see you've been really concerned about this test. I've found that when I get really worried about something, I find it difficult to ask for help. Is there something I can do to help you with the test?"

These statements not only begin with a validating statement, but they also let your child know that you've been paying attention, and you know what's going on in his life. They acknowledge that your child is the one in control of his test preparation, and that you have faith he will do well in this responsibility. After your child hears and understands this, don't you think he'll listen to your suggestion?

Remember, more often than not, our children act the way we expect them to. After all, we've been the most frequent contributors to the store of experiences and impressions that make up their self-concepts. Our children act, as we do, consistently with their self-concepts. If we talk with our children in a way that communicates our respect and trust in them, they will act in a way that merits it.

CHAPTER NINE

Self-Image

Lindsay, a terrific kid, a smart kid, attended a great private school. Lindsay's dad called to set up tutoring appointments, hinting that his daughter might need quite a bit of work.

The morning of Lindsay's first appointment found me, coincidentally, at her school, meeting with Joel during his study hall. As Joel and I were wrapping up, a friend of his, a girl, stopped by the desk to chat. "Well," she chirped, "I'd better go. I'm off to fail my history test." Now, I couldn't just let that go without comment. "What about, 'I'm off to ace my test?' What about thinking positively?" I asked. "It's just easier this way," she responded with a grin. "This way I'm not disappointed later."

That afternoon, guess who showed up for Lindsay's appointment? The girl I'd talked to just that morning at school! "How'd the test go?" I asked. She held up the test in triumph—"88!" I couldn't help wondering how well it would have gone had she been confident going in.

The funny thing is, if you listen to kids, they usually tell you exactly what's going on in their heads. The tricky part is really listening. I decided to take a roundabout tack with Lindsay. I explained that in my experience, sometimes people who talk negatively about their abilities are indirectly responding to feeling criticized. "Is it possible," I asked, "that there's someone in your life who may have been a bit critical of you lately? A coach who's been riding you, a sarcastic friend, an ill-tempered sibling?" Lindsay looked confused and thought for a moment. "I'm sorry," she said finally, "I really can't think of anyone."

We discussed other things for the remainder of the session. When Lindsay's father arrived, I walked out to introduce myself. "Hi, I'm—" I started, but he cut me off, blurting out: "So, does my daughter have a bad attitude, or is she just really dense?"

I was stunned. To me, it sounded brutal, but Lindsay was unfazed, continuing to pack up her workbooks. "Well," I fumbled, "we haven't really covered those issues; we're looking at other factors right now."

The next week when Lindsay came in, I very gently brought up her father's comment of the week before. "Oh, he was just kidding," was the reply.

People act in accordance with their self-image. Period. You can read about it in any pop psychology book you want, or you can take a look around you for evidence aplenty. I knew that Lindsay's father wasn't really kidding; I knew that Lindsay knew he wasn't really kidding; I knew that Lindsay's test scores would reflect this knowledge.

Lindsay's practice test scores climbed steadily: 630, 670, 690. She was getting excited. She had the hard evidence of a stack of practice tests substantially higher than her PSAT score. The day of the test, however, something happened. She came back with scores that were virtually identical with where they were before. Her subconscious mind brought her right back to where she was in the beginning.

The whole idea of self-image strikes a lot of people as mumbo jumbo, but it's a common idea for people who have done sports before. Lindsay, for instance, was a softball player, and very good apparently. She understood how to succeed at sports. You don't go up to the plate and think "I'm going to strike out," and then be happy if you don't. You go up thinking "line drive, right up the middle," or "high over left field, over the fence," and then you do it. Athletes have to have enough ego to think, "I'm the person who should be hitting the ball." Lindsay was really comfortable with that idea in sports. Why didn't it work for her in academics?

I think one of the real challenges is that our ideas of intelligence are so intertwined with our ideas of self. In other words, what we think of our minds is so much a part of what we think of ourselves—"I'm a pretty smart kid," or "I'm kind of a dummy." And because our concepts of intelligence are so integral to our concepts of self, they are much harder to change. A coach can teach me to throw a ball and I can separate that from who I am, because that's just a skill for a game and all games are learned, not innate. Sure, some people are born athletes, but anyone can practice hard enough to learn to throw a ball. Intelligence is so much more tied into self-concept that we can't think of it that way. Instead of thinking, "Oh, great, the coach is going to show me how to be a better baseball player," we think, "The reason my mom/dad/teacher/tutor is telling me this math tip is because I am stupid and can't figure it out on my own."

So Lindsay could overcome her previous limitations with sports but had a hard time doing it with academics and the SAT. She had already gotten the message from someone, somewhere, that she wasn't smart enough, and that was that. As she said, it's just easier this way, because then she's not disappointed.

It's funny, because as kids we absorb all kinds of information from our parents—beliefs about morals, money, politics, etiquette, and so on. Later on, as we receive other information in different ways, we change our minds. We read a *Consumer Reports* and decide that American-made cars really aren't always better, or we finally go ahead and try oysters despite parental warnings and find them delicious. It's easier to have those kinds of ideas changed by other voices or other life experiences because we can see how those opinions could be changed. They are opinions about things or people exterior to ourselves, not opinions about ourselves. Once saddled in childhood with the idea that you are, say, an exceptionally bright child, or exceptionally dull child, or an exceptionally mediocre child, you'll have a much harder time disproving that to yourself.

So a coach can fairly easily get you to rethink ideas about your sporting ability by teaching you discrete skills. But a teacher will have a much harder task in getting you to rethink your talent for mathematics, because that hits on your intelligence and that's just too integral to the sense of immutable you-ness. If you were an average student in kindergarten, it only makes sense that you'll be an average student in first grade, and on. And if the SAT measures smartness (which, by the way, it doesn't), then naturally you're going to be average on that one too.

And here's poor Lindsay. At a conscious level, Lindsay swept the negative comments aside and ignored them, but at a subconscious level, I believed they were sinking in.

Lindsay had incredibly negative ideas about herself and her abilities as she walked down the hall saying, "I'm going to go fail this test." And despite that stack of sky-high practice test scores, Lindsay went into the SAT and scored exactly the same score as she had months earlier on the PSAT. Why did she score so much lower than her demonstrated potential? Hearing her in the hallway at school that day planning to fail her test, hearing her father call her stupid, I couldn't help but assume it was because she planned to fail all along.

Best-selling author Malcolm Gladwell talks about the locked door in the mind, an area we can't access consciously. He asserts that many of our decisions are made there, in the dark, behind that locked door, and we can't always explain why we've made the choices we've made. That door, he theorizes, contains such entities as gut reaction, fear, intuition, and I'd add, all the forgotten incidents that make up self-concept.[1] For Lindsay, taking a guess about what's behind her locked door wasn't too complicated, but for many other kids, the "back story" of their beliefs about themselves is just as locked to me as it is to them.

Some of the kids I've tutored tell me their own stories, in various ways, over the course of weeks and months. Others won't and many others can't. Many of them don't know those stories, and many of them can't access them because it would be too frightening to face them. As in the case of Lindsay, some beliefs have to be suppressed to be held safely. I could see that Lindsay had those negative thoughts about herself, but pinning them on her dad wouldn't work because it was too scary for her to accept that. All I could do for Lindsay was to replace the self-talk at least for the hours during the test. That, and hope that a successful SAT experience would help to counteract the negative thoughts that were dominating her self-concept.

I had another student, about that same time, who had an entirely different story to tell about himself. Mike was, according to his mother, his teachers, and anyone else who chanced to assess him, a dumb kid. He'd never go to college—that was crystal clear to his mom, and cheerfully reported to me. Mike couldn't break 500 on the critical reading section. He just wasn't bright enough, and it wouldn't happen. I never saw a kid with so little parental support for his ability.

Mike was different, however, because on a deep level, he was coachable. His subconscious was open to suggestion, and his personality invited instruction. In other words, Mike believed he could learn the stuff. When I told him he could get a 550, and he could go to college, he accepted me at face value, and buckled down to work. Three months later, he brought me his score: 550.

Not only had Mike believed me that he could get a 550 on that test, he had replaced all the negative messages in his head with "Ned says I can get a 550; I'm going to get that 550." Taking that message into the test gave him, with remarkable precision, his target score, simply because he believed that he could.

***

Most of the time, underperformance is a mystery. Parents frequently tell me that they were surprised by their child's PSAT score; surprised, that is, because it was much lower than it "should" have been. The child himself seems as bewildered by the score, especially if he can't point to an obvious incident of anxiety as explanation. For a child who does well in math and in English class, it can be not just confusing but demoralizing to receive a substandard score on a test that supposedly measures intelligence and ability. Getting that lowered PSAT score is not just informative of a problem; it also manages to compound that problem at the very same time.

Take the example of Desiree, who is one of literally hundreds of students I've tutored with this problem. Somewhere along the line, Desiree got the idea that she wasn't good at math, and she performed according to this belief on the PSAT. Her verbal score nearly hit the roof, but her math score settled somewhere in the basement. Desiree, however, was taking precalculus as an eleventh grader and earning a highly respectable average. The math on the SAT never climbs above the most basic algebra II concepts, so why was she tanking the math section?

In this book, we often refer to belief systems. The belief that the SAT measures intelligence. The belief that the SAT determines where you will go to college. The belief that some people are good readers and some aren't. The belief that success is reserved for those lucky few who do not experience anxiety. Uncovering and debunking some of these hindrances to performance not only helps an overwhelmed and underconfident student perform better on the SAT, it also strikes at some of the deeper issues that feed this lack of confidence. We don't just want Desiree to raise her math score, we want her to be able to do that herself the next time she finds herself underperforming in any arena.

Here are three more students who learned to overcome problems with their self-images. These are the easy cases, with stories open to our view. The tougher cases are the mystery underperformers, like Desiree, where some detective-work, some guesswork, and some faith are required to make that push to victory.

Javier was a very bright and charming kid, a wonderful kid, who couldn't have done less if he tried. Week after week he brought me excuses for undone homework and attempted to divert me from the task at hand. I pulled out every trick I could in terms of playing motivational speaker—what are your goals, what excites you, etc. He was basically determined to say nothing. He was a really talented soccer player, but chose not to put out the minimal extra effort to be on an elite team. Instead, he just kept coasting at a secondary level. I couldn't figure it out.

Both of Javier's parents stopped by the office the night before the test. They were concerned because Javier was trying to talk his way out of taking the test the next day. He felt that he was unprepared and argued that it would be useless to try to take the test. As I began to address this issue, Javier's mother suddenly swooped in. In a tone of voice utterly unconcerned with my presence, Javier's mother delivered a thorough and unsparing dressing-down to her son. In front of me, Javier's mother made him feel that he was two inches high. Her basic message was that Javier would, despite Javier's and my concerns, be taking the test the next day.

What I realized was that this was the pattern of Javier's life. His mother was critical up one side and down the other in an unsympathetic, unloving way. What Javier heard repeatedly was "Son, you're a big zero." The safest way for Javier to protect his ego was to do nothing, because it was better to do nothing and hear "son, you're a zero," and think "sure mom, whatever." That was quite a bit easier than to put himself out there with his best effort and hear that wasn't good enough.

Grace started prep in the spring of her junior year, working for several weeks with another tutor before suspending tutoring and declining to take the SAT at all. A strikingly attractive young woman, Grace told her mom that she simply didn't feel comfortable with her tutor, that he made her feel stupid. Her mother asked me if I could make time to work with her.

Grace had a fine mind, but suffered from what my colleagues and I refer to as "pretty girl syndrome." Her perception of herself, her self-concept, was based on her looks and figure. Both were striking but pretty darn irrelevant to her SAT and college aspirations. She was bright—really bright—but she kept voicing fear of taking the test, fear that she would do terribly. She had scored 670 and 530 on her Verbal and Math PSAT. She had a good average, but her mindset was one of underperformance.

I asked what the issue was with the other tutor, who had "made her feel stupid." "Can you explain?" I asked. "I think he thought I was an airhead." There you had it. She needed the SAT to prove she was smart.

With any question she got wrong, I asked her to talk through her mistake, what had happened. Her language carried the classic clues of searching for validation. The solution was a constant expression of how well she was doing, applause for her effort, and respect for her intellect.

"You're such a geek!" I'd teasingly declare at every strong performance. She responded well. She beamed. She seemed thrilled to be "smart," to impress by her performance with no need to be cool, to be pretty, to worry about her image. Her practice scores were terrific. Her final SAT scores? Verbal 710, Math 760. She was offered academic scholarships to three schools, admissions to all seven schools she applied to, and settled ultimately on Colgate. She may well be the prettiest geek at Colgate next year.

Brooke is the darling, shy daughter of a successful and prominent attorney. Her older brother is gregarious and confident, and attends an Ivy League university. When I met Brooke for an initial meeting early in her sophomore year, she would barely look up from her lap. Her mother spoke for her. "Brooke finds this," or "Brooke is not like her brother in that way," or "Brooke struggles with this." Much of her mother's description of Brooke could be called explanation and was couched in comparisons to her older brother.

She returned at the end of her junior year to begin learning about and preparing for the PSAT. Hidden under wispy bangs and a shell of quiet insecurity was a formidable mind. It seemed her mother had never looked. Her mother constantly probed for how Brooke was doing, always score-oriented. I did my best to give her appropriately positive feedback that still left Brooke some space without having her shoulder looked over at every turn. "She's doing great" and "she crushed her homework" were met by surprise. Really?! Brooke would roll her eyes exasperatedly as her mom said "Now Brooke, it's just that I know this stuff is hard for you."

Brooke's mom asked if it were possible for Brooke to score as high as the 600s. "Actually," I responded, "I think she should aim for 700." Brooke's mother was astounded and delighted. Brooke's reaction was more complicated. She seemed clearly to relish her sense of her ability and my confidence in her, but there was an undercurrent of sadness of someone who has been underestimated and perhaps undervalued.

The point that stuck in my craw was that when Brooke's mom's eyes sparkled, it seemed to be for the scores, not for Brooke. I don't think she saw this in herself, but I know Brooke did.

SELF-CONCEPT AND PERFORMANCE

Why do students underperform? In some ways, the answer is extremely complicated, in others, quite simple. People act consistently with their self-concepts. We act in ways that harmonize with what we think of ourselves. And that goes for testing as well. Good test-takers do well on standardized tests such as the SAT, and bad test-takers never do. Every student knows which category he fits in.

For instance, if my sense of myself is as an athlete, I will be interested in sports, will play them, will talk about them, and will dress like a jock. If my sense of myself is as a student, an academic, I will take an interest in school, likely be bookish, engage in "weightier" conversations, and care what opinions my teachers hold of me.

All of these things are good and healthy. The problem arises when acting consistently with my self-concept has undesired consequences, when I adopt ill-advised behaviors or unwisely eschew others. If I think of myself as a jock, and my concept of a jock is a person who is not academic, I may neglect studying. I may lower my expectations of myself in school. I may even malign my classmates who are academic. "She's such a geek," or "He's a loser" (for being academic and not athletic).

As these ideas become part of my regular self-talk, they preclude my best efforts in school. I won't try as hard; I'll give up easily. Basically, I'll underperform. Then, those experiences become my consistent reality, simply confirming my sense that I'm not a scholar. But that's OK, because I'm a jock.

Now, if I'm a self-perceived "student," I may easily be intimidated by sports. I may give up before I even really try. I see more athletic students and figure I can never measure up. It's unlikely to occur to me that my classmates may be better at soccer because they've spent hundreds of hours practicing, that they don't simply "have it" and I do not. It's probable that I won't even think about those possibilities. I am comfortable in my geekiness and I just stay where I feel secure.

The interesting part comes if I do try to achieve outside of my regular comfort zone. Do I succeed or get pulled back to my old place? And if I do crash back to ground zero, why does that happen? Much of that is because of my self-concept.

Why We Tell Ourselves to Fail

For Javier, Grace, and Brooke, failure wasn't just an option; it was the path they knew, and that others had helped them discover. They didn't wake up one morning and decide, "I want to fulfill everyone's negative expectations of me." More likely, they just got tired of fighting against those expectations. Javier no longer had the energy or courage to try to prove to his father that he was a worthwhile kid. Grace wasn't sure that if she did well on the test, people actually would take her seriously. And Brooke was fairly convinced that she would never be able to measure up to her brother.

What's more interesting than these kids not feeling capable of success is the fact that they were not expected to succeed. That's a pretty confusing message. Javier, Grace, and Brooke all knew what it meant to do well, to make good, to succeed. They also knew that no one expected them to do that, and so, in a way, no one really wanted them to do that. No one was really pulling for that to happen. In a way, they weren't *supposed* to succeed.

And so, even if these turned out to be the most remarkably introspective and intuitive kids around and they figured this out, the barriers to success were at least twofold: the surrounding and sometimes oppressive expectations of those around them, and their own subconscious beliefs about themselves. It's one thing to throw off the subtle messages others are giving you and to succeed despite their expectations. It's quite another to succeed despite your own internal messaging and your own expectations.

Delaying Failure

For a person who does not see himself as successful, procrastination can be a very handy tool. After a long bout of procrastination, he can make a last minute Herculean effort, fall flat on his face, and then say, "Well, that was the best I could do—I stayed up all night—what else could I have done?" In other words, "See? I'm a failure, no matter how hard I try. Leave me alone."

Procrastination is a great way to put yourself in a position that preserves your self-esteem, protects your ego, and sabotages your goals and highest potential. If I really were absolutely set on my goal, I'd make a long-term plan and work persistently and consistently to give myself the best chance of doing well. But instead, people essentially paint themselves into a corner by forgoing the opportunity to do more earlier on and consistently. They then do the best they can at the last possible moment and predictably go splat.

Procrastination allows people to justify themselves—"I did everything I could"—to themselves and to their parents. It also allows them at a subconscious level to think "Well, that probably wasn't the very best I could do, maybe I'm smarter than that, but who'd ever know." There is nothing more frightening than doing everything you can possibly do and still coming up short. Most people don't have the courage to do that or they recognize that it's just not safe to do that.

Using procrastination therefore helps someone preserve his self-esteem, even when he's being told over and over again that he is a failure. The danger of this method is not just that it almost never leads to success; the danger is that the façade gets thinner and thinner each time the procrastinator uses it. He soon forgets that he can change.

CONTROLLING THE SUBCONSCIOUS MIND

Although psychologists and psychiatrists may use different terms, essentially we all have a conscious mind and a subconscious mind. Our conscious mind holds all the thoughts we can choose, our daily experiences and reactions to those, and our conscious memories. Our subconscious mind is the vast repository of experiences and beliefs that we cannot consciously access or examine.

The subconscious mind is like an internal organ that is affected by my conscious health choices. My heart has a lot to say about what length and kind of life I'm likely to have. It is very much affected by decisions about smoking, exercising, and eating well. It, in turn, can have a lot to say about what I can do. If my heart is in shape, I can run and hike and swim. If not, it can put the brakes, if not the lid, on certain pursuits. Some of that potential is also predetermined; there are hereditary factors that interplay with my conscious choices.

Now if we imagine our subconscious minds to be like our hearts, we can choose how we think about ourselves. We have choices about how we react to situations. Those thoughts and reactions are received by our subconscious mind and reside there. Our subconscious then works to bring those dominant thoughts into reality. If I have a constant stream of thoughts like "I can do this!" my subconscious mind will do everything it can to make that happen. My subconscious mind can bring answers to me, things "locked" behind that unexaminable door that I once knew but cannot actively recall can be brought to me in a dream or a sudden flash of inspiration.

On the downside, the subconscious mind can also forbid me from doing things, from trying things and succeeding. If I've constantly indulged in thoughts of failure and incapability, my subconscious mind is perfectly able to soak up those thoughts and use them as a barrier to my success, should I attempt something previously thought impossible. As in the cases of Javier, Grace, and Brooke, the mindsets of others can dramatically affect my subconscious assessment of myself and my abilities. And if my subconscious mind tells me no, it takes a supreme effort to override that decision.

Focusing on Success

Left to its own devices, my brain is a bit like a small child—easily distracted. The basic relaxation technique of picturing yourself on a beach, hearing the waves, feeling the breeze is really a study in displacement. If I am now seriously contemplating whether I want the pineapple or banana drink with the little umbrella, I will have a hard time simultaneously contemplating the plane crashing, filling out my taxes, or taking the bar exam. Where we choose to put our focus matters.

So, we want to do our best to control our thoughts, to steer them in positive directions to keep them from drifting in negative ones. The problem, of course, is that the subconscious mind wants to help out in every situation. It's always there and has a lot to say. Grace may have felt very motivated to get into Colgate, but getting her self-destructive subconscious in line with the project was a project in itself. It can take a while to get a deeply held belief system overturned, or even temporarily side-lined.

This is why displacement plays such an important role. In test-taking, we want to clearly visualize our desired outcome as well as the processes and techniques that create that outcome. I coach my students to imagine fitting their expert knowledge to the topic presented on the day of their test and to imagine getting a top score on the essay. I insist my students use specific techniques on specific math and reading questions for two reasons: (1) to get them to approach the test or question with structured and systematic methods to make the questions easier to do; (2) to prevent them from thinking about how hard the test is or about how they might do poorly, since their attention will be consumed by focusing on the prescribed methods.

I instill techniques in students to displace negative thoughts, to figuratively leave no space in their brains for anything but the knowledge and processes they've adopted for the purposes of this test. If Javier is busy following the routine of a technique I've advised him to use, he can't really spare the attention to his subconscious, which may still be sending out constant messages that he's not good enough. Not only is he working through the test in a more systematic and effective way, he's simultaneously suppressing the negative messages that have hampered his performance in the past.

Lindsay, whose father thought she'd never do well on the test, proved to have her fair share of natural intelligence and a surprising talent for math. The techniques I taught her were just the ticket to get her mind off the fact that her father didn't think she could succeed. Additionally, each time she successfully applied one of these techniques, she was indirectly combating her subconscious belief that her father was right. In this way, she built up a resistance to her constant self-disparagement through distraction, while at the same time proving to herself over and over again that she was eminently capable of rocking the test.

Stemming the Tide

Because the subconscious is a repository of basically everything we experience, if a lot of bad stuff has been dumped in there, it can take a while to counteract that. If I have received a lifelong diet of love and affirmation, I am likely to feel good about myself. If I feel good about myself, I am likely to behave in ways that bring me more love and affirmation. Unfortunately, the reverse is also true.

Teens who have self-images that are negative are likely to have those beliefs because of a mix of experiences, genetics, and other factors. Sometimes it's reasonable to find the causes and address them, sometimes it's not. If my negative self-concept is because of a lot of negative treatment I've received, it can be helpful to see that. To some extent most of us think we're no good at something because we've been told we're no good at it.

The most likely source of this is unhelpful comments (intended or not) from parents. Parents have a tremendous impact on what their children think about themselves and the world. Parents impart morals, religious beliefs, political convictions, and attitudes about money, gender, and race. Of course, children often ignore or shed many of these beliefs as they grow older. The hardest ones to shed are the ones we absorb about ourselves. It's easier for me to objectively believe that dad is wrong in his beliefs about the president when I read two books by separate authors showing why. It's much harder to do so with beliefs about myself. Brooke may have accumulated many successes in school to counteract her mother's opinion, but because her mother's opinion had become so central to her sense of self, she could not recognize her successes as such.

Moreover, beliefs about the self are like stereotypes—not easily changed. And, actively or not, we constantly search for reinforcing proof. If I believe all teens are bad drivers and I am nearly killed by a maniacal driver who appears young, I say to myself "See? Another one." If the driver looks to be my parents' age, I'll likely just label him an idiot of no particular group if I have no other stereotype of bad drivers.

Visualize Success

I worked with Lacey for the SAT, and she recently returned as a college senior to take the GRE. She had taken many practice tests in pencil and paper form, but her final practice tests on computer (the GRE is offered in a computer-based format) showed inconsistent and disappointing scores. Lacey was discouraged and confused.

We talked about the differences between the two forms of the test and between practice and actual tests. We discussed how the earlier pencil-and-paper practice tests were an actual indication of her ability. She protested that the most recent scores were more real.

"Well," I said, "we want to think of your scores as the range of your potential. If you've score 750 then you have the ability to get a 750. That doesn't guarantee that you'll get that score, but it does show that you have the ability to get that score."

After a while, it seemed that we had gotten her to feel comfortable with this idea, with herself, and with taking the test the following day. As she walked out the door and I was wishing her good luck on her test, I asked her to call me as soon as she got the scores. (On a computer-based test, test-takers receive their scores immediately after completing the test.) Lacey replied, "Sure, unless I don't do well."

Screech. Wait, wait, wait. I pulled her back into the office.

"Lacey, you are a wonderful person with a great mind and I think you are just terrific. Now, if you tank the test, you are still a wonderful person with a great mind whom I think is terrific and who has to take the test again. If you crush it, as I expect you will, you are a wonderful person with a great mind whom I think is terrific and who can do a victory dance on the GRE and not take the test again. OK?"

Lacey looked doubtful.

"Look," I said, "I know you can do it because you have done it. But you've also scored 200 points lower than that golden score. What's the difference? Sometimes it's the vocabulary words on the test, sometimes it's careless errors, and sometimes it's the luck of the day. We want you to take the test in a way that you score as much of your considerable potential as possible."

We then talked about her subconscious mind and how she could get it to work for her, not against her. We talked about visualizing victory, not fixating on failure. I think part of her thought I was a flake, but because she had already gone through the SAT with me, she listened. After a while, she seemed to be *really* listening. Finally she said yes, she could focus on her goal and not her fear, and she walked out the door.

I heard two days later from Lacey. 730 Verbal, 740 Math. A little belief sure helps. Visualize what you want, not what you fear.

Reinvent Yourself

Remember Brooke, who lived in her parents' and brother's shadows? Her case was one of the most difficult I've encountered, but neither Brooke nor I gave up. She learned 250 words faster than any other student in my experience. She responded so well, I believe, because the vision I held of her and that she held for herself when we worked together was eminently more inspiring than the one her mother held of her or what she felt about herself while she was with her mother. With me, she was made to feel brilliant, charming, and successful. At home, she felt limited, awkward, and young. Like the child who is a cowed middle child at home but the social dynamo of her group at school, sometimes people can reinvent themselves.

Most of the time, however, we need someone who can help us see what we can be. Brooke didn't immediately envision herself as a standout but took readily to the role when she caught the vision. And the last couple of years of high school are a great time for reinvention, the kind of reinvention that can see a kid well into the college years.

V

Overcoming Underperformance

CHAPTER TEN

Incentives to Succeed

High-stress parents usually think it takes high-stress methods to get their kids to work hard and do well. When the kids slack off, they increase the pressure. When the kids start to falter, they increase the pressure. When panic attacks come, they again increase the pressure. As hard as these parents are pushing, they are steadily making it harder and harder for their children to succeed. In fact, they are giving them incentive after incentive to give up. If only a 2100 will do, but I am only capable of a 1950, I may say "nuts" to the whole thing, doing nearly nothing, and settle for an 1800, rather than putting it all on the line to still suffer inevitable criticism for a 1950.

I've seen kids mentally check out of the process, realizing that's the only way they can survive. I've seen kids deliberately bungle practice tests, hoping to convince their parents to back off. I've seen kids choose to join the marines right out of high school after years of standardized testing and college applications. These kids somehow believe that only through sabotaging or opting out of the entire process can they get their parents to tone down the pressure or leave them alone.

It can be very frustrating for the parents as well. The harder they push, the more the kids resist. Even kids who sincerely want to respond to the pressure they are feeling, and want to respond with increased enthusiasm and focus, seem instead to wither under the additional scrutiny and demands. It can feel hopeless for parent and child alike. It can seem as if giving up is the only option. While the parents typically don't take this route, their children often do.

***

Rachel was a really smart kid. She was interesting to talk to, she worked hard, and she earned great scores on her practice tests. I didn't worry too much about Rachel, at least not at first. While she wasn't an SAT superstar, she had her head on straight and was steadily increasing her scores. We worked on math, her weaker area, quite a bit, but from the beginning I sensed that Rachel had a pretty good hold on the test.

One of Rachel's great strengths was a quiet confidence and an ability to not let the test stress her out. She approached each problem rationally and calmly, and continued through practice tests with an unhurried and careful pace. She began by scoring well and slowly increased her scores until she felt ready to take the test. We scheduled one last practice test just to be sure.

The day after that final practice test, Rachel's mother was in my office. Her voice was so strident and her voice so commanding that at first I didn't notice a shrinking Rachel accompanying her. Rachel's score wasn't good enough, and instead of seeking the reason or working toward a solution, her mother yelled at me and yelled at Rachel. Rachel visibly wilted. In fact, her practice test score was in line with the gradual curve she had crafted and represented a solid increase over her PSAT. She had done the work necessary to get a great score, and she had been ready to take the test.

As was to be expected, things didn't go as smoothly for Rachel during that next week before the test as she and I had planned. Rachel's mother wanted success so badly for Rachel that she decided to take matters in hand, and insisted that Rachel be given several hours of daily homework leading up to the test. Instead of feeling confident and composed, Rachel began to appear careworn and anxious. Most importantly, Rachel began to care less and less about the SAT. Her anxiety was not associated with the SAT, as her mother may have assumed, but with the constant failure she experienced in comparison to her mother's demands. By the day of the test, Rachel seemed to have given up altogether.

Parents often feel that the more important the goal, the harder they should push. Well, I agree. It's important to give the SAT proper attention. After all, it is one of the major factors that admissions officers weigh in determining whether your child will be admitted to their universities. The problem I see with so many high-stress parents is not the intensity of their desire for their children's success; it's the methods that they use. While meaning to do the opposite, far too many parents are simply failing to provide their children with any real incentive to overcome the SAT.

Rachel had managed to stay calm and focused on the SAT despite a myriad of external stressors. She knew she had pushed herself about as far as she safely could, and she felt happy about her accomplishment. When her mother demanded better and provided a grueling study schedule as insurance, Rachel lost all that she had gained over the steady months of preparation. She knew that an unreasonably large number of practice tests wouldn't bump her score up but were likely to increase her anxiety.

Although Rachel was already giving this test her all, faced with her mother's demands, she realized that her all would not measure up. She might as well give up, which she did. It helped her anxiety slightly but failed to increase her score to the level her mom wanted. As might be expected, Rachel's score on test day dipped below her practice test potential. Rachel was past caring.

Too often, parents assume that because so much pressure is associated with the SAT and inherent in a timed standardized exam, their children will understand the importance of the test and respond with their most fervent attention and their best work. For so many kids, however, all this pressure and stress fail to create reactions with meaningful or productive direction. They know the test is scary; that doesn't always mean that they're going to try their best. They also "know" all sorts of misinformation about the test and its importance; that doesn't make them better at taking the test. It's not enough to be cowed by the test; kids need to be invigorated, motivated, and directed. They need to actually desire to do well on the test, and further, they need to actually know how to do well on the test. They simply need those basic incentives.

It's our job as parents, tutors, and teachers to provide that direction and to hone that motivation. The SAT makes everyone want to do *something*—the trouble is, lots of time that something is either to *worry* or to *run!* Worrying is not preparation, and running only gets you to your goal if you are sure you are headed in the right direction. We want the SAT to make your child want to buckle down, concentrate, and really shine. And you can help make that happen.

We all need basic psychological incentives to work hard and perform well. When each victory counts for itself, a child feels that their effort is worth it and is noticed. That recognition will make the child want to go for another victory. Having defined goals gives us structure so that it makes inherent sense to work hard, as does praising the actual qualities that make up success, not the outcome. Rewarding and recognizing qualities makes the kid want to work on those qualities more. Other psychological incentives include treating a lack of success not as failure but as feedback, so fear of failure doesn't overwhelm the desire for success, and allowing the child a share in her destiny—she's incentivized to work hard because she helped devise the plan for working hard. She wants to get a good score because she knows what that means for her future, and she wants that future.

For some teens and some families, all of those healthy incentives are already naturally there. For most of us, however, it's worth making sure that our children understand the test the way we want them to understand the test. For most, an incentive structure overhaul is the easiest way to rechannel all of that inevitable SAT stress into focused and productive ambition.

KNOW WHAT THE SAT IS ALL ABOUT

The SAT should not be just one more vague, unknowable step in a terrifying process. Its level of importance should be quite clear in your child's mind. Be clear. Give information, and make absolutely sure it's accurate. Give the SAT its proper place so that your child understands that it's an important test but not a life-determinant test. When your child understands exactly what role the SAT takes in the college admissions process, he'll be able to gauge for himself how much importance to give it, as well as whether it's wise to allow himself to have fear about it.

So many parents assume that fear is the only potent motivator out there, and if their child isn't scared witless by the test, then he'll blow it off and wreck his chances at Princeton. The truth is that most of those parents are expressing their own fears for their child's failure, and guess what? Their kids are always bright enough to understand that. In my experience, a teenager who sees that her father is terrified that she'll fail the test is typically neither motivated by his fear nor, needless to say, buoyed by his lack of confidence in her. Knowledge is always fear's antidote and provides a much more healthy and productive form of motivation.

Fear whispers, "What if you fail?" Let your son know what happens if he "fails"—either a retake regimen or other options, such as the ACT, colleges that don't look at SATs, a transfer plan after starting at a less ambitious school. Having a defined plan for when things go wrong actually acts as an incentive to make sure that that plan doesn't have to jump into action. Instead of having a generalized fear of failure with all of the uncertainty that can bring, a kid can understand that if he doesn't hit his target score, then he'll have to gear up for the next SAT and do it again. That's a nonterrifying incentive to get this whole testing thing over with as painlessly and quickly as possible. In other words, do it right the first time, and you'll avoid a lot of extra work.

When your child understands what this test is all about, he'll also understand that it is in his best interest to do well. Remember when your kid was five and refused to put on shoes to go on errands? When your kid understood that the planned destination was the park or a friend's house, those shoes went right on. Your teenager hasn't changed that much. He still feels obstacles are either insurmountable or not worth his time when he's not interested in the outcome or reward. When he has an interest in success, he buckles down. Knowledge is power: when your kid understands this test, he feels more assured, more confident, and more sure of his victory. When he feels more confident, he'll want to show that off with a stellar score.

You may be asking yourself if this is really necessary. A complicated incentive structure just to get a kid to study for a test he should already know is important? You know your son. When he really wants to do something, his determination can seem inexplicable. We want your son to really want to do this and do it well. We want his motivation to come from within—a constant sense from the child himself that he wants to push himself a little bit more and do a little bit better. It's just a whole lot more effective than a parent's most monumental effort to outwardly motivate that unmotivated child.

SEE HOW TO DO WELL

The SAT doesn't require guesswork. This test has been around for so long and has been analyzed and parsed so many times that there's really no excuse to not find out how to do well on this test. There are thousands of books on the subject. There are dozens of available practice tests. There are teachers, tutors, and gurus aplenty waiting to educate you on this very subject. There is no need for guesswork or assumption. Find out how to do well on the test—and make sure that your child knows.

If you don't happen to already be an expert on the best way to snag a top score on the SAT, go ahead and tell your child. Say, "Now, I really don't know the best way to go about this test. It's a different thing than I do at work or than your sister did two years ago. Let's get some expert advice." This shows your child that you know the test is a big deal, and a new kind of big deal. It also shows your child that you're in this together, and that you'll get the help he needs to make sure he gets his best score. It tells your child that it's perfectly acceptable to ask for help, and that you're not going to second-guess any research he does on his own.

Finding out how to do well on the test may seem obvious, but it's an important part of your incentive structure. This makes sense—there is no incentive to do something you don't know how to do. Imagine pointing a child toward the laundry room and saying, "Now get all these clothes clean!" He won't even try; he doesn't know where to begin. My daughter, however, who is two, has been shown how to pick up dirty clothes, one t-shirt at a time, and throw them over her head into the washing machine. She loves doing this because she knows how and can be successful.

Teenagers are the same way. There is enough about typical life in high school that is overwhelming or unknowable; life is constantly changing for a 16-year-old. Chances are your son or daughter is like most people and loves to do things that he or she is good at. Show your child how to be successful, step by step. Don't hand him an SAT registration form and say, "Raise your score by two hundred points!" Hand him a vocabulary book and say, "Let's try the first lesson together."

Teenagers love to feel successful—we all do. We enjoy playing the sports that we're best at. For most of us, choosing a career is as much, or more, a matter of proficiency as inclination. We like our jobs because we're good at our jobs. By the same token, doing anything repetitively that we're bad at is an experience in frustration and is bound to lead to distaste for the activity. How many times do you want to go to the driving range if you can't hold a club properly, much less hit the ball off the tee?

I've seen otherwise disengaged students start to really enjoy the SAT once they understand how it works. As my students increase in ability, they increase in enthusiasm. I had one particularly gifted student who worked some 50-odd practice tests, asking me to hunt up more. Once she learned how to be successful, she never wanted to stop.

So how do you incentivize your child to study for and perform well on the SAT? You make sure he knows how to study, and you make sure he knows how to do well. With those key elements in place, he'll be much more likely to want to study and to want to do well. And it snowballs: the better he does, the more confident he'll feel, and the more he'll want to study and perform. Confidence equals success, especially on the SAT.

No Failure, Only Feedback

"Feedback is the breakfast of champions," Ken Blanchard wrote.[1] And that's just what a low score is—feedback. If your son *should* get a 600 on his math, and he *does* get a 600 on his math, well then, that's great! For others, a 600 may seem an unmitigated disaster; it's a low score compared to their abilities. Either way, it's feedback.

Treating it as feedback can be hard. As we've discussed, the SAT is not a measure of who your child is and certainly not of who you are. Maintaining that perspective is not easy. But as discussed in the chapter on communication, if you want to change a score that is below your son's potential, you need to know the facts, and getting as much information from him as possible is unquestionably crucial. Getting as much information out of that "low" score is the best way to change what looked like a defeat into a step on the way to victory.

Parents who hover over their children or their children's tutors, anguishing over any dip in practice tests, are creating a fear of failure not conducive to success. Students need to try different processes to see how they work. They may have taken an early morning test after staying out too late with friends. Their giggly friends may have been making faces or text-messaging them during the test. They may have overslept and not had breakfast. Only by treating underachievement not as failure but as feedback can you get to the causes behind the results. And knowing the causes is indispensable to discovering the cures.

A Shared Destiny

When your daughter participates in a plan for her future, she is much more likely to invest in that plan. She chooses why she wants to do well, and where that great score she's planning on will take her, making her really want to get there. Give her a reason to want to succeed and make sure it's a reason that is important to her. That's the only way she will be really motivated.

The SAT should be one step in a larger plan that your daughter has created or fully supports. She should be able to see the steps that came before and recognize her part in making those happen. She should be able to see the steps that come after, in order to not unduly emphasize the importance of the SAT and therefore its anxiety-causing potential. All of this should give her both a healthy perspective and faith in herself.

Additionally, a plan she is committed to should provide an unwavering motivation to continue the course that she mapped out so carefully and that she has followed successfully for some time. She should also be able to see that throughout her journey, not every step has gone as planned, but that she has learned from and assimilated the feedback she's received, developing flexibility and resiliency that will serve her well on the SAT.

Popular media is full of dramatic stories of children being pushed into unwanted majors, schools, and careers. In the movies and on TV, we're given examples of terribly overbearing parenting and its results. Most of us (correctly) would claim that we are nothing like that. While we may not be the domineering unsympathetic monsters we see on the screen, we influence our children in other ways, all sorts of ways, without always realizing it. Our kids may not know about schools or careers that fit their interests or skills, unless we help them find them. Our kids may be influenced by our subtle value judgments of different kinds of workers or people, and feel that they cannot choose those lifestyles or careers. Our kids are often a lot more naïve than they usually let on, for they cannot know what they do not know. They may have chosen not to assert themselves about their futures as much from ignorance as from fear or intimidation. When we make the effort to help our children discover futures and opportunities that excite them, we motivate them on a profound and lasting level.

As importantly, your child needs to feel responsibility for her future. Failure to take responsibility is endemic in our society and runs roughshod over our children's potential. It's failing them. It's jailing them. It's taking away any hope they had in a bright future. Start now to give them responsibility. Use the SAT as a laboratory for them to practice running their own lives. Give them a reason to own up to their problems and limitations, and they may just find a reason to overcome those problems and limitations.

I tutored a very sweet and perceptive young woman who was dealing with a significant learning difference. Trina's academic abilities were limited to the point that she had learned to rely on her father's direction and an obliging personality to get through high school. Unfortunately, the SAT proved to be quite a different challenge. Trina blithely and obviously cheated on her SAT homework in a way that revealed to me the depth of her disconnection to the reality of the test. She simply did not feel that scoring well on the SAT was something that she needed to worry about or take responsibility for.

Trina attended a school that gave her great grades for being functionally illiterate, and she knew full well that her dad had her future all planned out. When it came down to putting her pencil to the Scantron answer sheets, she used a mixture of guessing and good-natured faith that things would turn out just fine for her. It was clear and painful to me that Trina had no concrete concept of her future and no sense that it was her responsibility to craft one. That, more than any score, however low, was the real limitation on Trina's future.

When you hand your daughter the reins, her self-concept will soar. Let a toddler sit in the driver's seat of the car, and he feels like a race-car driver. For a teenager who is presumably past that illusion, putting her behind the wheel, literally or figuratively, is still a deeply affirming and motivating experience.

Part of the Team

It's so incentivizing to feel like you're on a team. Use inclusive pronouns when you talk about SAT preparation: "We're going to find you a great tutor," and "We'll study vocabulary every night after dinner for ten minutes." Just a simple switch of pronoun can help your child feel like this project, while his responsibility, won't have to be faced utterly alone.

If it fits your child's personality, find him a study buddy so they can schedule together and motivate each other. Left alone, most of us will procrastinate. Having someone to report to or to goad us along helps to ensure that those promised tasks really will be completed. Half the reason people pay for personal trainers is simply to have someone to be accountable to lest they skip another week of exercise. Don't ask your 16-year-old to be more mature than most adults. He'll have no reason to be a go-getter.

Now, let's be honest. You know your child. She is not the most organized creature on the planet. Even if your kid is surprisingly on top of things for someone her age, she's still someone her age. Don't strain her limits. Don't expect her to multitask like a top executive or to budget her time like a partner in a law firm. She needs assistance, and not just a day planner. She needs structure, both overarching and hour by hour.

As discussed earlier in this chapter, that structure must be at least partly devised and implemented by her. She must feel in control of the study schedule, but you can help her to make sure that there *is* a schedule. WARNING: do not take this as permission to micromanage your child's life. This is terribly disempowering for any child and a major disincentive to taking responsibility. Think of yourself as your child's administrative assistant, rather than as the boss. "Just a reminder that the report is due in two days" will be better received than "You better have that done by Friday, or else!" Give her charge of her destiny, but assist her in accomplishing her goals by sitting down together and planning her schedule.

Be part of the process, but don't *be* the process. Your child should always feel that he is on a team, and that it's a team that not only wins but is designed to win. There's literally no way to lose when you're on a supportive and forward-looking team, where setbacks are only feedback and winning is not a matter of if but when.

Praise and Celebrate the Effort

Too often, we save our praise for the end of the journey and use it to measure outcome, not to influence results. Praise is a powerful tool and an unmatched motivator that should be used unsparingly throughout the process. Praise can turn discouragement into victory. A child who receives steady praise for good habits and progress has every incentive in the world to redouble efforts and increase the rewards.

Praise the effort. Applaud her studying vocabulary in the ten minutes before *The O.C.* comes on. Tell him "Thanks for getting your homework done on time." "I appreciate your coming home a little before curfew so you can be rested for your SAT class tomorrow." In sports, in music, technique matters. Practice matters. Months of lifting weights and hours of practice take place before the game or the performance, and that takes encouragement and support. With the SAT, we should applaud all the habits and efforts that contribute to doing well. Praise the effort and good results will follow.

Find increments to measure the progress that your child is making in preparing for the SAT. Give him near-constant encouragement as he works toward his goals. Express faith in his ability to overcome every SAT obstacle he confronts. Better yet, actually have faith in him. There's nothing more empowering than someone who believes in you.

How many times do we tell two-year-olds, "You can do it! You can do it!" when all we want them to do is stack some blocks? When these kids grow up, too many of them don't hear that encouragement very often anymore, but they are facing much tougher challenges and have a much greater need for the leg up that encouragement so often brings. Praise the efforts and the results may surprise you. And remember that positive encouragement is still being absorbed into their self-concepts and own self-talk. If all they hear is "You are doing great. You can do it," that's likely to be the tape they play in their heads the day of the test.

SET UP SUCCESS

The SAT just isn't a win-lose situation. It doesn't prevent anyone from going to college, from becoming botanists or cardiologists or sculptors. The SAT is only part of the process. Someone can still pursue a PhD in economics if she attends an SAT-optional school such as Bowdoin or Bates. The SAT is but one criterion of college admissions and only for schools that require it. And, it doesn't guarantee anyone admission anywhere, much less ensure that he'll graduate and make something of his life. It simply doesn't have the power to set the tenor for the rest of a child's educational and professional career, although at 16, it can sure feel that way.

Make the SAT a win-win. Make sure your child understands that there is literally no way to fail the SAT. Help him understand that success is inevitable because failure is undefined. After all, there is no SAT score so low that it can prevent a person from becoming a success. If assured of victory, your child will want to keep going, even after setbacks. If he knows that no matter what happens, he succeeds just by taking the test, he knows that the SAT is a test worth taking.

So how do you make the SAT a sure victory when there are obviously numerical values pegged to each attempt? Celebrate the benefits of the process. Recognize that as your child is building SAT skills, he's also building discipline, the ability to handle stress productively, and a college-worthy vocabulary. Reward his optimistic attitudes, his willingness to give it another try, his eagerness to conquer something difficult, and his refusal to give up. Compliment the progress in those measurable, achievable goals, and the other goals will follow. Don't make this about one four-digit number—let him know that you're proud of what he's done, not what he scored.

Second, don't talk about "if." "If you do well" means there's a way to lose. "If you do well" means there's a specific number that signifies victory, and anything falling below that might as well be zero. "If you do well" means your child probably won't. You *can* use "when." "When this is over, won't we all be so proud of you?" "When you get a chance to put all this practice to the test, you'll be surprised how good it feels." "When you're in college, you're going to have a great time." "When" means certainty and assures that however difficult the present may be, the future is better and getting closer all the time. "When" means you really believe that everything will be all right in the end. With determination, hard work, and parents who care, everything really *will* be all right in the end.

If you set up the right incentive structure, almost anyone will do almost anything. It's a sure victory. But part of creating the right incentive structure for your children is making it easier for them to do well on the test than to bomb it. You've got to make it easier to be successful than to be a slacker. For most of us, that seems impossible without using nagging and hen-pecking, but in reality, that's usually the worst way to go about it.

When a teen has committed supportive parents who believe in him, he finds it easier to be a hard-working, successful student than not to be so. After all, to not study, to not do his best, means that he has to metaphysically squash down all that good will and positive energy sent his way. He has to say to himself, "My parents believe I'm a great kid, and I want to prove them wrong." He has to take this fabulous gift he's been handed—belief in his worth and ability—and chuck it away. That's not an easy thing to do.

After all, each of us wants to believe that we are important and capable and worthwhile, and we wanted this even more as teenagers. If that affirmation that is so dearly desired is being constantly offered from a loving source, kids aren't likely to entirely push that away. They need it too badly.

Making it easier to do well than not do well means setting up a situation in which a kid's self-image is of being successful, and then watching him act consistently with that concept. This kid won't be someone who is motivated to become a better person; he'll be someone who sees himself as a successful person and acts in accordance with that self-concept. When it comes down to it, we all act in ways consistent with our self-concepts. We have to.

A majority of the kids I tutor claim to be self-motivated, but I maintain that the truly self-motivated child is extremely rare. The truly self-motivated child is the one who selects a destiny radically different from his background and with great personal struggle achieves it with no family support. So what motivates all those kids I tutor? Fear, for the ones from unbalanced families. The well-adjusted ones? The well-adjusted kids have self-concepts that require them to be successful.

My student Ayala felt superior, partly because her parents felt that she was and they were superior people. She felt that her education was superior and her teachers were superior and her mind was superior, and she didn't hesitate to admit that. It wasn't arrogance, it wasn't bragging, it was fact. She felt that she had a superior mind and a superior future, and she did not let a little thing like inferior SAT performance change her mind about that. And you can be sure that her great confidence in herself and her SAT skills gave her the motivation to keep working until her SAT scores matched her high opinion of herself. You know—she was right all along.

Ultimately, a great incentive structure is one that helps a child feel superior and helps to give him a self-concept that includes inevitable success. When a child believes that she is a successful person with superior abilities, she acts in ways that bring that concept to reality.

Every one of the incentives outlined above do just that. They tell a child who he is in relation to the SAT, and they tell that child that the SAT is nothing compared to his brilliance, hard work, or perseverance. And when a child understands that she is smarter than a test can measure and that she is destined for greatness, that child has every incentive in the world to squash that test in her haste to move on to better things.

CHAPTER ELEVEN

Confidence

Rodney was, I'm sorry to say, an insufferable kid with a superiority complex. When he nabbed his 1410 on the old SAT, he made sure everyone knew it. And the one person who could never forget was Rodney's sister, Miranda, younger by just one year. Rodney made sure to lord it over Miranda on a near-daily basis, in keeping with his practice of insulting and disparaging her intellectual ability, appearance, and weight. Miranda's parents were almost no better, withholding praise and generously dispensing criticism whenever possible.

When Miranda came to my office, with her 1210 score and downcast eyes, I got mad. Mad at Rodney, mad at their parents, and mad at anyone and everyone who had contributed to Miranda's belief that she wasn't good enough, or as good as her brother. Working with her for just a short while, I came to believe strongly that Miranda was just as intellectually able as her brother. I made it my mission to prove my theory.

Accordingly, I enrolled Miranda in SAT boot camp. I had her working harder than she thought she was capable of, and I made sure she knew that I didn't doubt her ability for a second. As her skills grew, her confidence grew. As her confidence grew, her scores increased. And through it all, I worked hardest at replacing the tape recording in her head, the one with the constant refrain that she'd never measure up. I encouraged her. I praised her. I commended and *applauded every positive step she made. I told her over and over again that she would nail this test.*

When her SAT scores came back, Miranda and I each had one of the most profoundly satisfying moments of our respective lives. For her, it was a personal victory that would change the tenor of her endeavors and family relationships forever. For me, it was the epitome of tutoring success. For the score Miranda brought home was not just as good as Rodney's, it was better. 1420.

Confidence is about belief. No kid walks into my office without a strength of some kind. I have never worked with a single kid who was utterly devoid of talent or ability. And yet, I have tutored so many kids who felt worthless. Somehow, ability hasn't created confidence. They don't yet believe they are capable. I have worked with student after student who, despite financial and educational privileges most of the world can't imagine, feels incapable of achieving any kind of success. Preparing for the SAT when a student feels worthless is not starting from ground zero; it's starting way, way behind.

On the other hand, when a confident kid walks in my office, I know how likely it is that we'll hit a home run. When I work with confident kids, I can throw them bizarre concepts, convoluted tricks, and paradigm shifts and they'll catch them one-handed. For a confident student, there are almost no limits on the score he can achieve.

The funny thing about the SAT is that it's really not such a difficult test if seen the right way. The difficult part is getting kids to see the test in the right way, and that requires confidence. The SAT is not an achievement test. It's not an assessment test, or even an aptitude test. The SAT is a mind trick, filled with many individual mind tricks. Think about it—in order to achieve a nice plump bell curve, the SAT has to convince capable students that they're not. It has to be able to fool smart kids with solid grades. And it does so, year after year.

In order to see the SAT as the psychological trap that it is for so many students, it requires confidence. Not confidence on my part; I'm plenty confident in my SAT skills. It requires confidence on the part of the student—confidence that no matter how the SAT skews information he knows, he can still make a slam-dunk. If he believes that, there's a good chance that he will. If he doesn't believe that, then there's a good chance the SAT will claim another victim.

And, believe it or not after the stories shared here, there are plenty of parents out there who are giving this gift of confidence to their children on a daily basis. There are parents who are diligently working to provide their children with the opportunities and examples they need to develop their own sense of confidence. I've even worked with kids who were wildly overconfident, which I love to see. While it's all too easy to break someone down, it's incredibly difficult to do the reverse.

The SAT rewards confident kids with plumped-up scores. Confident kids see more testing tricks. Confident kids work more quickly and don't get discouraged when minor setbacks occur. When I send a confident kid out to take the SAT, I know that there is much less standing in the way of his target score. He will have obstacles that he knows he can overcome; he will not have insurmountable barricades. When I send out a kid who hasn't quite reached a solid level of confidence, I'm on pins and needles until the scores come back. I know that any minor incident before or during the test has the potential to sink that kid. And all too often that happens.

***

I worked with two smart twins, brother and sister, who possessed very different strengths from each other. With siblings, it's extremely difficult to not compare abilities, especially on standardized tests. With twins, it's practically impossible. While Beth in many ways was intellectually superior to her brother, Max had a knack for the kind of math that baffled her. Max also had the bluff confidence common to teenage boys, while Beth shared the shaky diffidence of so many of her female peers. Coincidentally, the twins, through very different skill sets, had the potential to reach nearly identical target scores.

I knew Beth's lack of confidence would be the deciding factor on test day; her practice tests were wobbly, dependent on circumstance. When she felt good, she performed well; when she felt unstable, her scores dropped. I prayed for a good morning that Saturday in April. I waited for her phone call that afternoon.

Beth was despondent when she called. "I was hyped up and ready, and feeling great, and we all sat down to eat a good breakfast, just like you said we should. Then Max noticed that I was a little nervous and started joking about how much my pencil was going to shake during the test. My mom jumped in and said something really

condescending to me about keeping my chin up even when I started
doing badly. That's when I lost it—she said when I did badly, not if.
It was like my own mom was betting against me. I was so upset I
could hardly concentrate on the test."

One idle, thoughtless comment, and Beth went under. The next
time she took the SAT, she had her typical level of self-doubt to deal
with, but in addition, she carried the knowledge that she had already
tried and failed. Her uphill battle just got that much steeper.

The week before the SAT, my colleague's student fell down the stairs in
his family's house. He suffered a few fairly serious bruises on his legs
and arms. He was lucky.

His mother contacted my colleague to review SAT procedures for
special accommodations as he had injured his writing hand. After she
gave her the information and inquired as to her son's well-being she
said, "All I could think about when I saw him start to tumble down the
stairs was 'Oh no! All that money we've spent on tutoring!'"

Think of the confidence deficit this young man had to contend
with as he limped his way to the testing center that day. Not only was
he working with a sprained finger and sore ribs, but he knew that his
mother was expecting defeat. Think of the delicate structure of confidence that Beth had erected in preparation for the SAT and how easily
it crumbled. This chapter will discuss ways to build a different family
culture than the ones these families lived with.

From the way you speak about your children, they learn what you
think of them. From the way you act, your children understand their
chances of survival and success in the outside world. From the way you
guard them, your children learn what they are capable of. From your
thoughts, your words, and your actions, your children are educated to
their own limitations.

TALK THE TALK

Too many parents fall into the conversational habit of focusing on our
children's weaknesses. We complain about our toddlers being picky
eaters and unconsciously reinforce this behavior in them. Whether our
reasons are to appear humble or to highlight the heaviness of the
parental burdens we carry in order to garner sympathy, a habit takes

hold. All too soon we're complaining that a son reads sports magazines but won't pick up a "real" book, or a daughter needs a pricey tutor to keep her up to speed in math. What didn't work on our toddlers certainly won't help our teenagers either.

Talking this way becomes a habit. After all, we don't want to appear to be bragging about our children, especially when we may actually worry that our kids are inferior in some way. As parents, we are supposed to instruct and correct, and how can we do that if we fail to identify problems in behavior or ability? Remember, complaining about our toddlers didn't make them want to try the broccoli. Similarly, your child won't test well until she feels that she is a person who does well on tests. Reminding her otherwise will only exacerbate the problem.

Try to turn this around. Try to speak of your child's strengths as positively as you can. When, conversationally, you would ordinarily state your child's limitations, instead find a way to state his strengths. It won't be as hard as it seems. Instead of "Jim's completely unreliable," try something like, "Jim's got a lot of spontaneity," or "Jim's full of surprises." Instead of "Kathleen's always been a terrible reader," try either "Kathleen prefers math," or "Kathleen works really hard on her reading skills." You will be surprised by the difference—not just in what others hear, but in how you start to think about your child.

When you speak of your child's strengths, instead of his weaknesses, your mind starts to change its focus. Even when you are consciously, even awkwardly, forcing yourself to speak positively of someone, your subconscious mind begins to follow suit. You will begin to think of the strengths first, before the weaknesses. You will start to feel more confidence in your child.

What's more, your child will feel the difference more quickly than you think. I cringe when a parent drags a reluctant child into my office, declaring loudly the intellectual failing that necessitates the tutoring. I'd give anything to hear the list of virtues before the recitation of faults. While a parent gives me the opening speech, I'm already calculating how long it will take me to undo the damage.

On the other hand, when a child hears her parent talk about her strengths, she is always buoyed and further strengthened. She will start to understand that her parents believe that she is capable. The next step after this realization is the growth of a belief in herself that she is, actually, a capable person. And so often, after that, she becomes that capable person—the one she was always capable of becoming.

Parents would argue, "But Lizzie has always struggled with math," or "Tim actually is a very poor reader." That doesn't matter. Not only does saying so make it worse, but those terribly damning opinions of a child's abilities simply don't always apply to the SAT anyway. The fundamental thing most often misunderstood about the SAT is that it does not measure intelligence. It does not measure ability. It does not measure aptitude. At least it does none of these things with enough precision that we should trust it to measure something as significant as our intelligence, aptitude, or academic attainments. It's one test on one day. Moreover, it's a blunderbuss, not a rapier. There are few false positives on the SAT (guessing one's way to a perfect score is a virtual statistical impossibility), but there are many false negatives (many, many students find all sorts of ways to score less than they should). Whatever your child's academic profile, the SAT is not the test to give you evidence enough on which to base proclamations of his ability or lack thereof. So, no child should feel incapable of achieving a solid score, because no child lacks the ability to learn how to take the SAT. It matters little what reading group your child inhabited in third grade or how her geometry grade turned out. The SAT is an entirely different measuring stick. Let your child start fresh.

Interestingly enough, as we've been discussing, probably the most critical skill required for SAT success is confidence. It isn't a gargantuan vocabulary—that certainly helps, but isn't enough on its own. It isn't an A+ in calculus—in fact, knowing too much math can actually hurt a student's chances. These underlying skills matter in the sense that if recognized and touted, they create a belief, an expectation, of success. Keep in mind, however, that not knowing every word or math theorem is not an anchor on your child's potential. I continually tell students to make decisions on the basis of what they know, to use the tools they have. The ability to think creatively and apply what you know is the most useful skill any student can bring to bear on the test, and that is impossible to do if that student doesn't have the confidence to take a shot. You may not be able to directly implant vocabulary words into your child's mind, but you have quite a lot to say about the level of confidence your child possesses on the day of the test.

WALK THE WALK

Kids who aren't confident in themselves usually don't come by that naturally; they've learned it somewhere. One student told me in all seriousness that her whole family tested poorly. She started from such a confidence deficit that it was nearly impossible to pull her up to a positive level. Too many kids inform me that their parents were awful test-takers and that it must just run in the family. And, as discussed previously, what kids believe, they become. Confucius himself observed that we are what we think. Kids who feel that they are scatterbrained typically have either learned those patterns from parents who can't seem to keep track of the tutoring schedule or, perhaps more importantly, who have a running self-talk of "I'm such a ditz" or the like. And, as you might guess, really confident kids often have parents who are either, themselves, really confident people or people for whom praising and encouraging is a matter of course. After all, success breeds success. Well, actually, success breeds confidence, which breeds success.

Please be open-minded when you try to assess success, either for yourself or for people around you. It's too easy to assume that confident parents equals financially successful parents, parents who stand out in their careers or who have some socially significant reason for feeling so confident. This, surprisingly, doesn't seem to matter. In fact, kids whose parents have lucrative and successful careers run just as high a risk of becoming less confident simply through a perceived increase in pressure to achieve. The girls who prance in with Prada bags and Mercedes keychains are just as likely to go one way as the other. I've tutored the children of people I'd be thrilled to get autographs from, people whose incomes are hard to imagine, but their kids seem just as susceptible to self-doubt. It isn't the level of success a family reaches; it's the level of confidence a family exudes.

Conversely, it can often be the parents who are less than wholly focused on their own careers that are the more able to impart confidence to their offspring. They are confident in who they are, their beliefs, the choices they have made. These parents may be more apt to demonstrate, and allow their children to participate in, a more balanced lifestyle. With less of a family focus on financial markers of success, these families can give their children a better perspective on some of the overly significant academic markers of success, such as the SAT.

Again, it's not the income of a family that matters; it's the lifestyle balance that a family reaches. It's what they believe in. If you take nothing else from this book, believe in your children's ability to achieve, to persevere, and to succeed. And let them know that you do.

People often question why this generation of students is so uptight. Why are there so many anxiety attacks, eating disorders, and general stress cases among our high school students? The reasons are vast and complex. Some are societal issues, hard to control, things "everyone is doing." The fast-paced world of more and more and faster and faster is hard to opt out of. The reality that, for the past decade, each year has been the hardest year ever to gain admission to college cannot be changed. The rise of high-stakes testing—whether the overblown role that the SAT now plays in admissions and the popular psyche or the national standards in the No Child Left Behind Act—has not made any of us or our children more at ease. Parenting magazines abound with stories of multitasking teens, madly overscheduled. From the rising competitiveness of high school sports to the increasing competition for internships, extracurricular activities, and private lessons of all sorts, teens are living as fast-paced lifestyles as their parents.

High school students themselves blame it on increasing competition to win top slots at top universities. They claim that much of their drive stems from a need to create an impressive resume for their college applications. Most of my students assure me that they are inwardly motivated to achieve, and that they are just doing what it takes to survive. They wouldn't do it differently even if they could.

Yet we continue to see the panic attacks, the meltdowns, and the increasing illnesses and injuries that result from overexertion in the classroom and on the lacrosse field. It isn't fear alone that compels them to rise at five each morning for swim practice after studying for biology long past midnight. It's a lifestyle they've adopted, and one they've often been observing at close quarters for most of their lives. The high school students of this generation are living in a society, and perhaps in a family, that consciously overworks itself. Children learn how to behave at home.

But there is one significant difference: for most of us, if we are lucky, we have gotten to choose our lives and our lifestyles. If we want the bigger house, we may choose to work more. Want a lower golf handicap? Practice more. We are adults; we get to make choices.

Choice imparts control. People feel content and confident to the degree that they feel a sense of control. Part of our job as parents is to slowly give our children a little more rope, a little more leeway, a little more of their own control of things. "I do it," is my two-year-old's current favorite phrase. So I let her, to a degree. No, I don't let her drive the car, but I let her help pour the milk, even though I know she will spill it. But remember, anything worth doing well is worth doing poorly, at least the first few times. She has to learn at some point and that involves making mistakes. We have to give many choices to our children along the way—ideally when ramifications matter less—so they can develop the sense of control that is integral to confidence. At the end of the day, confidence is nothing more than an unshakable sense that "I can handle this. I can do this. And, if I blow it, I can handle that too."

When prepping kids for the SAT, I routinely show them an easier or better way to do this or that problem, only to have them insist that their way is better. "Good point," I'll say, "then let's do it your way and then give this other way a try. That way, when we get to the test, you can decide which is right for that particular situation. If we can practice both ways, then you'll have a second method in case the first method isn't right for that situation." This approach sure takes patience. But, it's not my test. I'm the coach, not the player. I don't play the game or take the shot. I can certainly demand that students do things my way, and they will. For the brief hour they are sitting in front of me. After that? It's back to their own way. The control needs to be in their hands.

If we want our kids to become successful adults, they must practice being adults, and that means making choices. Now, I can hear a lot of you thinking, "That's all well and good when you are talking about a little spilled milk, but this is my son's future." And you'd be right; it is his future. His. At what point do we let kids exert control over their own lives? When do they get to be in charge? That would be a great SAT question if the SAT had open-ended questions and covered philosophy. The answer is a trick: there is not one point at which you can say that's it—he's all set; *now* I can let my son be in charge. But parents who try or wish to control or orchestrate their children's lives risk doing so forever, sending messages all along the way that their children really cannot do it on their own.

I have a friend whose mother told him in his senior year of high school, in all seriousness, that she had no idea how he was going to succeed in college without her. First, what a horrendously disempowering message that is. Second, if she had been trusting him all along the way, then she would have been watching him handle things (mistakes and all) all along on his own. So, walk the walk. Do not tell your children that you trust them and then literally or figuratively take responsibility out of their hands.

Do not do their homework for them. Ask them if they would like help. "Want me to proofread that essay for you, Joe?" And let it be okay if he says no. Let them make their own mistakes. Did he get a B- on that one? Gently ask again the next time, "Want me to proofread that essay for you, Joe?" But be sure it isn't, "You'd better let me proofread that essay since last time you got a B- when you did it by yourself." Help him learn his own lessons. There is no better source of learning.

It's been my observation that people seem to learn from their own mistakes only. How wise we might all be if we really could learn from the mistakes of others. Unfortunately, we generally don't. Your kids are not likely to learn from your mistakes. All those painful stories from your youth that you hope your kids will learn from—they all carry less weight than what your kids experience here and now. It's just the way it is.

And, even though in so many ways our kids seem to be fully functioning adults, taking on more responsibilities gracefully than we may remember doing ourselves, they are not yet adults. We cannot force our choices on them without shooting down their confidence. It has to be okay for them to fail, to come up short, to look around to see how things might go differently the next time, and then to see that we are still right behind them. They need to hear us saying, "That's okay. You'll get it next time." Our children will benefit immeasurably by our confidence in them. Even if you find yourself currently frustrated by your child and his lack of success, know that your belief in him will do more to make him successful in the future than anything else you might do. At the very least, your lack of belief in him will do more to limit his success than anything else you might do.

If what we want is to raise a generation of young adults who are confident, independent, and successful, then general busyness is neither the problem nor the solution. One of the most salient commonalities I have noticed among confident, independent, and successful children is that a great proportion of them have confident, independent, and successful parents. Why? Well principally, success begets success, because, again, success creates confidence and confidence breeds success. Those parents who appreciate and build upon their successes, in any arena, tend to expect success in other areas as well, and so are teaching their children to believe their own skills and abilities.

Whatever your particular level of career success, whatever your field, whatever your hours, interests, and hobbies, your children are learning from you. At the end of the day, it may not matter if they adopt all or part of your lifestyle choices, or consciously reject as many as they can. What matters is that you showed them a way to live independently, happily, and confidently. If they start with those gifts, they won't need to spend the rest of their lives hunting for them. Incidentally, they'll have the wherewithal to score big on the day of the SAT.

GET OUT AND DANCE

One of the best ways I've seen to teach children how to be confident is to teach them success. Success naturally breeds confidence—after all, if a kid has already slammed the SAT once, he knows for a fact that he's capable of doing it again. What is success on the SAT? My students are successful on the SAT when they get scores that maximize their potential. The really fantastic thing about success is that it generally doesn't care where you get it from. If your child knows how to be successful in one area of his life, any area, he'll be more able to transfer success to other areas.

Remember Joe, the cross-country runner who learned all those vocabulary words? How did he know it was possible to beat the word game? He learned how to face an enemy on the track. He knew how to train for a meet. He knew it took determination, long hours, and more than a few hard aches and pains. And he knew, really knew, that he could win at that game. All Joe had to do was turn his skills to words.

Once Joe started down that familiar path of attack, the process was familiar to him, and he had the confidence to keep going. He knew what was at the end of that road: victory. He had confidence in the process of overcoming; he had experienced it before. Joe beat the SAT because he knew how to win.

And it isn't just the athletic kids who pick up that precious self-confidence along the way, although playing sports is a great way for your child to learn how to beat long odds. Students who play instruments, students who perform in dramatic productions, students who tackle giant research projects or hold down demanding afterschool jobs or coach Little League or excel in Boy or Girl Scouts—all of those kids are getting the opportunity to test their limits, push themselves, and experience victory. A lot of those kids are building up knowledge on how to be successful.

One of the critical skills that a child needs is how to risk, how to act outside of his comfort zone. After all, the SAT lies within the comfort zone of only a few, arguably somewhat unbalanced, people. Taking any timed standardized test requires a wellspring of confidence that has been fed by prior experiences in facing fear or intimidation. Providing your child with a variety of experiences and opportunities is a great way to help him build up that confidence.

I tutored a wonderful girl named Nina, whose SAT skills were spotty at best. She struggled with ADD, and often couldn't get herself to keep her mind on the SAT long enough to finish her homework. Math tricks would slip in and out of her mind, seemingly randomly, resulting in sometimes stellar practice tests, sometimes rather shaky ones. To be objective, Nina had no real reason to feel confident about the looming testing date.

Nina had something else, though, to keep her on task, something critical. Nina was a competitive horse jumper. For years, she had competed with the best in her class. She was a great rider and she knew it. In the face of skittish practice test scores, Nina didn't worry; she'd dealt with skittish ponies before. When her math skills slipped away from her, Nina knew how to regain control. Even in the midst of defeat, Nina remembered that no defeat is definitive, and that there will always be another chance to start again.

As Nina and I battled with the SAT that year, we never lost hope. With each setback, she renewed her grip and began anew. Through her equestrian training, Nina had developed a sense of her skills that was more optimistic, and more true, than the SAT alone would have given her. Without that sense, I have no doubt that the SAT would have been the one to declare victory, instead of the other way around.

What Nina's equestrian experiences and Joe's running skills, and so many other kids' different extracurricular activities gave them is essentially an anxiety bypass. Anxiety is, after all, the natural result of low confidence meeting an unfamiliar challenge. These kids had dealt with anxiety before. They had dealt with all sorts of challenges, fought all sorts of anxiety, and had eventually come out victorious. The next time anxiety threatened them, they weren't as apt to succumb.

As anxiety is the principal culprit behind underperformance, learning how to squelch it in the early stages seems like a pretty good idea. Each time your child successfully beats out anxiety, her confidence level will grow yet again. By practicing her confidence, she'll inevitably increase it, until anxiety becomes a puny threat at best. The familiar palpitations and racing mind will serve not to presage disaster, but merely to remind her of past victories. Her confidence will inform her actions, and her testing and SAT score will reflect that incalculable benefit.

ALL IT TAKES

It does seem surprisingly easy to think that all you have to do is impart confidence to your kids. They'll then take that confidence and use it to overcome any anxiety that threatens to sabotage their SAT skills on test day. It seems surprisingly easy, but it certainly isn't.

Teenagers are living in a world fraught with unbalances, stresses, unknowns, and anxieties. We live in that world ourselves. How we deal with and share this world with our kids makes a critical difference in how they choose to deal with it. If we can't seem to get a handle on our own lives, how can we expect that of our children? And yet, we do our children a terrible disservice when we elect to not show them the incredible capabilities they each have for success.

The quest for each of us should be to live and raise our children in a way that they will feel the confidence to attack any problem in front of them—be it geometry, ethics, or any other obstacle—and overcome it. All of that confidence starts at home. It shouldn't be surprising that it's the kids with confidence who know that they'll be able to figure out a way to crush the SAT.

VI

Planning to Succeed

CHAPTER TWELVE

Goals and Plans

If one does not know to which port one is sailing, no wind is favorable.

—Seneca

Too many kids come into my office not knowing what they want. Too many kids wait for me to take the lead in their test preparation, and answer my questions with blank stares. Mateo didn't even sign up to take the SAT, assuming that his tutor would take care of all that. Caylee had no idea where she wanted to go to college or what she wanted to study, making a target SAT score too much of a moving target. Too many kids are waiting for their parents or tutors or teachers to plan their futures, not getting invested in the process enough to realize that in the end, that SAT score is their own.

It is certainly not impossible to achieve success without goals, but it is much easier to do so with them. To begin with, what is success but achieving goals? Students will often ask me, what is a good score? "For what?" I reply. The answer is always, "Well, you know, a *good* score!" This is a mark of someone who has not clearly defined his goals, someone who needs a score to validate some nebulous and ill-defined idea of success. There's nothing wrong with trying to do as well as you can, but there is a danger in never being able to declare victory.

For some people, setting goals seems completely unnecessary. Obviously the reason Mr. Jones is dropping Jimmy off at tutoring every Thursday at four is to cause an increase in Jimmy's SAT score come March. Parents deposit their children, muttering "make it so" and head down to Starbucks, often without even wondering what kinds of steps will be needed to increase that troublesome average SAT score. At the end of the tutoring and testing experience, these parents are interested in one thing only: that hoped-for four-digit number. What they are missing is the opportunity to use the SAT as a laboratory for collaborative family goal-setting and achievement.

What good goal-setting adds to the above scenario is the chance for Jimmy and maybe his tutor to get on board with the program. Or, ideally, for parent and child together to determine what is important about the SAT experience, how important it is, and how they hope to achieve certain specific targets. These targets generally do include a specific score range but should focus more on the procedure Jimmy plans to implement in order to get there. As time goes by, Jimmy can attack the obstacles in his way and perfect his procedure, knowing that by so doing he is making it more likely that he will achieve that golden score.

You may already know what your kids want. Or, you may assume that they want what you want for them. After all, you've had a lifetime (theirs) of opportunity to instill in them your values, which include priorities of what it means to be a good or a successful person. You have pushed, cajoled, nurtured, and encouraged your children to be successful in the image you have of them or for them. Ideally, this has worked out swimmingly. Your kids have adopted your values and goals as their own and are currently working toward them. If so, sitting down to talk about goals will simply reaffirm a shared vision. If, on the other hand, the past several years have been marked by tension, conflict, and fights, it is possible you have been trying to push or drag your children down a path they don't want to go. If you are rowing in different directions, you are probably mostly going in circles with a lot of fruitless and frustrated effort.

DEFINE SUCCESS

Marla's mother had low hopes for her daughter. "Let's just see if she can get a 550 on the verbal part of the SAT," she said. "She's no word whiz." OK, so Marla wasn't actually a word whiz, but she worked hard, and at the end of a couple of months she was ready for the test. I hoped she'd have a lucky day, and she did. 610. In the standard SAT prep handbook, that's code for "declare victory."

Marla's mom didn't think so. If she could get a 610, why couldn't she get a 650? She seemed to have forgotten that despite Marla's hard work and lucky day, she was still no word whiz. Instead of celebrating Marla's victory the way Marla deserved, her mother declared it a failure and registered Marla for the next SAT. Marla, having seen just how her hard work and determination was rewarded, couldn't bring herself to put in the same amount of effort for the second test, and that day didn't turn out to be nearly as lucky: 540, and discouragement as well.

Too many kids have no idea when to say when, or what success looks like, so no matter how well they do, they still feel like they've failed. Their parents drop them off for tutoring, hoping they'll do better on the test, and then when they do, they hope to do better again. They tell me in September that a "good score" is above 1900, but in November, they're gunning for a higher score. While a sky-high SAT will never hurt you, the lost time and increased angst required to get there very well could.

Some kids have a specific idea of success that is either so far out of their reach or so far beyond their needs that it over-prioritizes the SAT, takes over their lives, and ensures failure. I've seen kids pin all their high school hopes on an SAT score, thinking that a magic number will secure their futures and give them the college education or career or sense of self-worth that they fear they cannot get on their own. I've seen the SAT claim all of a teenager's weekends and free time for years on end. I've seen the SAT become the most salient topic in a parent–child relationship to the detriment of not only the child and the SAT score but the relationship as well.

In other cases, some parents think so poorly of their kids that they set the bar too low and give their kids no motivation or confidence to try harder. Without a goal, these kids don't understand that they could do better and achieve more. Even if these kids beat their perceived score limitations, they know how their parents judged them and can't forget that. Usually, these kids either barely make the score that is actually well below their potential, or obey the subtle messaging to fail and bomb the test completely.

The tricky thing about the SAT is that, strictly speaking, the number scores mean a lot less than we think. In terms of the test-taker's ability, a 790 and an 800 are no different. Luck and the bell curve take care of that difference. The standard deviation for each part of the test is between 30 and 40 points, so that in theory, a 680 and 720 should be for all intents and purposes the same score. In fact, some of the SAT administrations have been scaled so punitively that the difference between an 800 and a 770 is just one point. That's one question you read wrong, or for which you missed a tiny trick, or just plain blackened in the wrong letter. On that test, for a student to have insisted on a 780 or above would have required her to consistently perform absolutely utterly perfectly for nearly four hours straight. That's not just unrealistic; it's statistically improbable. Defining success as a number is a dangerous practice.

Defining success is, in itself, setting a goal. We all want to be successful, so once we decide just what that means, we're essentially setting ourselves a mark. Be careful where you set it. In terms of numbers, I've found that in most cases—after assessing special needs, past prepping experience, and test management issues—setting a goal 100 to 150 points above a student's first few practice tests works. In other words, the goal is high enough to excite the student into working hard, and yet low enough to feel achievable and therefore worth working toward.

Once we've decided the number we're shooting for, we can focus on the more important goals, which always have much more to do with the things that can actually be controlled by the student. Study schedules, calming techniques, skipping strategies, math tricks, vocabulary methods—these goals are much more meaningful and productive than crossing your fingers and hoping for a number to fall in your lap.

The more important success to define falls in the realm of process. Students should feel successful and rewarded when they stick to their planned processes, following the guidelines that they know lead to success. I love to hear students tell me excitedly that they used smart skipping strategies, remembered to breathe deeply when they felt stressed, and back-solved the tricky math problems. When they are conscious of using successful strategies during the test, their confidence soars. They know they are beating the test. They've already overcome anxiety—by seizing control of the testing process, they have banished panic and set themselves up to increase in confidence, momentum, and accuracy through process as the test continues.

Those students knew they were successful long before the scores came back, because they had already overcome the main obstacles to success. For those students, waiting for the scores to roll in a month or so later is that much easier: They know that whatever the number, they've been successful. They also know the number will be right where it should be; they've done the test right. Far more importantly, they have learned an invaluable lesson on how to plan for and work toward success. They'll take that lesson with them to college.

DECIDE HOW TO GET THERE

It is crucial, and therefore difficult, to be utterly clear about your goals and yet remain flexible in the process. It's a natural tendency—we become comfortable with, and then wedded to, our routines. No matter that we experience failure over and over again. It's easier to face failure, after all, when you are comfortable with it. What is infinitely more difficult is to abandon faulty processes and face the possibility of danger without that reassuring crutch.

Most of the time, in fact, we don't even realize how irrationally we are behaving. We instinctively revert to these behaviors and often do not even know we've performed them. Think of nervous mannerisms, such as pushing your hair behind your ears or shuffling your feet. Clamming up in a meeting when you know it's your only chance to impress. Even when we know we're doing something, even something potentially self-destructive, we often don't know why.

One of the reasons we like to stick to our comfortable processes is that we've invested quite a bit of ego into the way that we do things. If I'm driving to the post office and trying to get there before it closes, shouldn't I take my usual route? But if my passenger continually berates my directional choices and insistently points out that *her* way of getting there is faster, what are the odds that I'll actually carefully weigh the merits of her claim? Of course I won't. I'll insist that I've been to the post office hundreds of times, and I certainly know the best way to get there. I'll keep insisting all the way there, even at the risk of not achieving my stated goal, getting there on time to mail my package. At the risk of failing at my goal, I'm sticking to what I'm comfortable with.

The SAT is a lot like that. Students say they want a 2400, and yet they can't seem to motivate themselves to practice. A mother tells me that she would like her daughter's testing confidence to increase, yet she repeatedly makes derogatory comments about her daughter's ability in front of her. A father tells me he's committed to his son dramatically increasing his SAT score, but after each tutoring session he comes in to argue with me about my tutoring methods. A student knows careless calculations are wrecking his chance for a perfect math score, but he still insists on doing speed math in his head to prove that he can.

If something is worth doing well, it's worth doing poorly the first several times. It's worth slowing down, writing out the steps, perfecting the process, and then working on speeding it up again. If what you're doing isn't giving you the results you want, as the parent or as the student, then it's time to start over with a different process. Let go of the habits that are leading to bad results and begin again.

First, challenge yourself to be okay with being awkward. Try watching the end of a movie, and then watch it afterward from start to finish. You'll see the film more objectively, because you won't be anxious to find out how it ends.[1] This idea works for the SAT as well—if students stumble and worry their way through math sections in terror of the final page, to break this reaction, as practice do the final page first, then go back. If kids get swept along in the critical reading passages and get lost in the morass of questions, pick one question out of the middle of the pack, answer it, and then pick another. Even something as simple as starting with the last answer and working upward can pull your mind out of a routine that hasn't been working for you.

As the parent, ask your child how he plans to study. Then get on board, no matter how different the process is. He'll be more likely to ask for suggestions or include you in later decisions. Find things to compliment and help him see which techniques are leading to good results. In fact, being complimentary and supportive is the most positive and productive way you can help your child reach his goals. Goal-setting with my students is easy if the student is self-actualizing. If he isn't, then we have to help him learn to visualize himself as a successful student; continually reminding him of his successes is the best way to do that.

Use Measurable, Achievable Goals

The surest way to ensure failure is to make success impossible. Success is impossible if it lies far above the potential of a student, and equally impossible if there is no way for a student to know if he has achieved it. Either scenario leads to discouragement and failure, no matter how the number score comes out.

The surest way to ensure success is to make it measurable and achievable. If you can see how to get there, and what it looks like, you'll be much more likely to put in the effort to make it happen. You'll also be more likely to declare victory when you've hit it.

If this seems like a lot of effort for an SAT score, think of it this way. This SAT score is something kids carry with them a long, long time. You still know yours, right? If your child feels like a failure at the time the score comes in, chances are pretty good that he'll carry around that feeling for a good part of his life, at least every time the subject of the SAT comes up.

And here's the kicker: It's not the score that defines success or failure, it's us. It's our parents' expectations and our older brother's score and our best friends' scores. I ask every student I tutor what he or she thinks a good score is, and it's a different number every time. The correct answer is: "A good score is one that allows me to pursue my education in the way I think will be best for me." Guess what? I've never heard that from any student. (I have, however, heard it from a few parents, and when I hear that, I know their kids are going to do just fine.)

So how do you ensure that your goals are achievable? The first thing is to not blindly set a number as a goal. Choose colleges to apply to that accept students in different ranges of SAT scores with programs that are exciting and interesting to your child. Have your child take a practice test and analyze it. Figure out where there is room for improvement, specifically, and how that improvement will come. Then set incremental goals based on process, not outcome. For instance: "I will not get hung up on particular math problems. I will read the passages more quickly. I will reread the questions so that none of my errors are from getting the directions wrong. I will not miss a subject-verb corre-lation question again. I will find three or more questions for which I can plug in numbers." Make those goals the benchmarks, and there is where success will be found.

Write It Down

Any book you pick up on achievement, whether for athletics or personal finance, touts the "magic" of written goals. Most of us have all sorts of wishes, ideas, and dreams. These, however, are different than goals. A written goal is a contract with yourself. The magic occurs in that writing down goals imprints them in your subconscious like nothing else. It sets your subconscious to work on getting the job done and also keeps you going when your enthusiasm flags. If your dream never leaves your own thoughts, then if you give up, no one is the wiser. With a written goal your subconscious will give you another dose of enthusiasm or a swift kick in the pants when you need it. At some point, we all need it.

In our office, some of our colleagues put this idea into practice as "The SAT Vow." A one-page game plan for the day of the SAT, it in-cludes standard fare about target number of questions, skipping strate-gically, and using this or that process for this or that type of question. The clincher is that, after reviewing the terms, we have students sign it. It's one way of making sure students perform as they have practiced, fo-cusing on the processes to get the desired outcome. But it's also a way of affirming to students that we have confidence in them—look, we are signing it too.

Give it a try. With your teenager, brainstorm ideas of what you can do to assist your child. Have your child write down what he or she can do. Remember to write down what *you* can do, not what your child can do. Goals are personal and so the actions behind them must be. Jot down, right now, a few of the goals you have for your child—more specifically, jot down a few of the goals you have for your relationship with your child as it pertains to the SAT. Sound tricky? Remember, base it on process, not on outcome. How do you want to act so that your communication regarding the SAT will be supportive and produc-tive for your child?

Ideas for your goals include: I will gather brochures for the types of colleges my child has expressed interest in. I will ask my friends what

GOALS WORKSHEET

_____

_____

_____

_____

_____

_____

_____

_____

_____

_____

_____

_____

_____

_____

_____

_____

_____

_____

_____

_____

_____

_____

_____

_____

preparation their children found helpful. I will be sure to ask my child about other commitments before scheduling time for an SAT class or tutor. I will offer to review vocabulary daily with my child, but leave the choice to my child. I will praise and encourage, trying always to find a gentle way to express my concerns and suggestions. I expect the best for my child and will treat my teen only in ways that support that.

Your son or daughter might write: I will do my SAT homework in advance, not during the car ride to my appointment. I will write down the specific things I want or don't want in a college so my parents know how to help me. I will ask my mom or dad to review my vocabulary with me with me daily. I will listen to hear my parents' advice as suggestions not as criticism. I will get a good night's sleep and eat a reasonable breakfast before my SAT and any practice tests. I expect to do well and will do only things consistent with that goal.

Make It Measurable

Writing goals down is also the way to make sure that your goals are measurable. My student, Linda, decided that she would always do eight out of ten sentence completion questions correctly. That's certainly measurable. She decided that in order to ensure that her goal was achievable, she would study vocabulary cards ten minutes a day and work on her sentence completion method. Linda then focused on the process she had decided on—studying vocabulary ten minutes a day— and was thereby successful in reaching her goal. By raising just her sentence completion percentage by 20 percent, she raised her overall critical reading score by 50 points.

Essentially, Linda tricked her brain into achieving a 50-point critical reading increase by accident. If she had started out claiming that she needed a score 150 points higher in just six weeks, fear of failure would have kept her paralyzed. Doing practice tests over and over again for six weeks would have given her the experience of missing sentence completion questions over and over again for six weeks, and she would have walked into the SAT with a tested conviction that she was no good at sentence completions.

Instead, Linda studied her practice test, found a few weak areas, and devised a plan to overcome them. She was successful at overcoming those areas before SAT day, and she knew she would be successful that day as well. Her subconscious mind didn't have a chance to sabotage her. She had already reached her goal.

This process works for parents as well as children. Parents can decide to improve positive communication with their children by adding four compliments a day. They can set aside ten minutes every afternoon to discuss how school went that day. They can commit to helping their child study vocabulary every evening after dinner. With small, measurable, and achievable goals, a lot can change for the better.

Manage Expectations

Part of setting goals is clarifying, codifying, and bringing to light the semiconscious desires we all have to be successful. If students can bring their spoken goals in line with their secret expectations, they can be much more successful. Many times, it is the unspoken goal that derails an otherwise promising testing trajectory.

For instance, siblings of high-scoring students may not ever state directly the pressure they feel to measure up. Close friends often foster a more rancorous SAT competition than enemies ever could, but more quietly. It's important to recognize these hidden goals because they feed a student's motivation and confidence more than some of the more outward incentives.

In other cases, the hidden goals are more process based. Many of my students, and especially the boys, feel a special sense of pride when they "don't need" to write out any math calculations, instead doing the reasoning and manipulations in their heads or on their calculators. Another large group of students require finishing each section early in order to feel successful. Others simply cannot allow themselves to skip a question, even at the risk of throwing the rest of the test.

To be honest, very few students are actually willing to do whatever it takes, legally that is, to get the highest test score possible. We are all too wedded to our own sense of process and control. The act of stating goals specifically, however, helps to bring these hidden process prejudices to light, and allows students to see more clearly what they may be doing to sabotage their own success.

Unfortunately, our hidden expectations are significantly more difficult to shed than the expectations we readily admit. After all, Susan may or may not get into Brown with a 2240, but she will always cherish the day she outscored her brother.

Along with uncovering hidden agendas, managing expectations requires monitoring a student's progress in achieving his goals. It's critical to recognize and communicate about growth and achievement. Talking about what a student is doing today, next week, and next month allows him to track his progress toward his goals and to note how his incremental goals are growing into a bigger success.

This process also flags problems early on and allows for adjustments either in process, in expectations, or in both. Let's say Tommy wants to score a 10 on his essay, but after a few weeks of work notices that he is consistently misunderstanding the essay question and writing off the topic. He now knows a problem area to work on and also is forewarned that he may need to beef up his multiple-choice score to cover a weaker essay tally.

Although I'd like to say that managing expectations mainly involves the students, the truth is that we as parents present the more formidable obstacle. It is, after all, our expectations that inform our child's sense of success and personal ability, and even the parents who attempt to hide their personal expectations for their child are rarely successful. I tutored one child whose mother tore up her child's PSAT scores without letting her see them, declaring that scores weren't important and she didn't believe in them. When she subsequently signed her daughter up for six months of top-notch weekly tutoring, her daughter got the message.

Keep It Personal

> The future belongs to those who believe in the beauty of their dreams.
>
> —Henry David Thoreau

Make the goals personal. No one jumps out of bed in the cold, dark hours of the early morning for someone else's dream. No great work of art was composed for the love of someone else's life. Your child must be selfish. She must imagine what she wants, and then dream it, plan it, and go for it.

With the SAT, though, this is really tough. First, the long-term academic goals of young people are typically really their parents' goals.

"My son's goal is going to my alma mater" is all the right letters, but like a good anagram may have a different syntax: "My goal is my son's going to my alma mater." Make sure that your son's goal is his own, or it's a good bet he'll give up on achieving anything.

Setting goals for SAT achievement should therefore be scrupulously particular to the individual student. I had a parent lecture me repeatedly as to how he had studied for the California State Bar Exam, implying that I should be instructing his son for the SAT in a like manner. It just doesn't work that way—for the test or for his son. The SAT is not like the real estate licensing exam, the driver's license test, or defending a dissertation. It's not even a whole lot like the SAT you took or your eldest child took. Your child will most likely best learn and study and achieve in a different way than you did.

I tutor siblings routinely, and often twins, where the temptation to systematize learning and goal-setting is ever-present but has, and would, seldom work. Have a separate and unique goal-setting session with each child and assess needs separately. Your daughter may need weekly sessions to reassess her goals; your son may need a written chart or incentive system. Goal-setting is personal. Remember that no one, your child included, is truly passionate about achieving someone else's goals.

I can't tell you how many times I've talked to parents about their child's goals and known just from the way they were talking whose goals they really were. "We'd like to go to Penn or a similarly situated school" is quite a bit different from "My son is considering Penn because he really likes urban schools." Allow your child to share in your dreams, but practice phrasing *his* goals as *his* goals, not as your own. He'll notice the responsibility and ownership you are granting him in his future. It is, after all, he who will be taking the test and doing the heavy lifting to prepare.

Keep It Positive

You can't plan in the negative. You can't have a goal to not have a panic attack, and it really doesn't work to decide to not run out of time, to not fill in the wrong answers, or to not get numbers mixed up in your mind. If you walk into the testing center repeating to yourself, "I will not be a failure as I was last time," what do you think your brain is registering?

Goal-setting is a positive activity, and goals are positive plans for the future. Goal-setting is forward looking and optimistic in nature. Goals must be set at a level above the currently achievable. Goals tell the subconscious mind that more is possible.

Sometimes I tutor kids who can't see beyond their disappointingly low performances, and I set goals for them. I study their past practice tests, I watch their methods and timing, and I tell them, "You can score 50 points higher in each section," or "My goal for you is to break 700 in math." They look at me, incredulous, but excited at the possibility of achieving scores they hadn't thought were within their ranges. Sometimes that simple statement alone is enough to break them out of a cycle of discouragement and its companion, underachievement.

Just as pointing out bad habits is much less efficient than beginning alternative, good habits (think of a smoker switching to chewing gum in order to help him quit), so setting positive instead of negative goals will help a child leapfrog over obstacles that were formerly daunting. Instead of focusing on the panic attack, the student is focusing on the methods he knows will be successful for him, and the panic attack never happens.

Be positive *for* your child, be positive *with* your child, and be positive *about* your child. When you are positive about the future, your teenager will be too.

Some of the students I tutor astound me with their never-ending and crushing workloads. Week after week, they drag into my office exhausted, overworked, and completely stressed about a major test they have to take the next morning. And then I bring up the SAT. For these students, especially the juniors who see no end in sight, it's critical that some milestones are celebrated. They need to feel progress, they need to hear praise, and they need the motivation to go on. More importantly, they need the confidence in themselves that being celebrated brings.

I want my child to feel great about his score, wherever it ends up. I had one student who took a math SAT exam call me up after he got his score screaming, "You are a genius! And I am a genius! A 420! I got a 420!" And he was serious. I could picture him doing cartwheels down the hallway. In his very specific situation, that score met his goal. It might have humbled anyone else, but for him it was precisely the score he needed. I can't control what my son's score will be, but if my son feels that he succeeded, he'll take that confidence and build a life on it. He'll take that to his college application essays, to his freshman English class, and to his graduate school examinations. If your child believes he is a good test-taker, he'll approach his entire future differently. Kids who feel great about themselves are simply more capable than kids who don't. They'll do better on the SAT because they believe they can. And they'll do better in life because they have already proven themselves to be winners.

So how do you stay positive? Think about those measurable goals and break them down. Did Ella get her timing down on the essay? Did Nate finally learn to implement plugging-in strategies on the math section? Did Laura get through an entire practice test without panicking? Identify small areas of success and talk about them. Give your child a tangible, identifiable piece of SAT success, and you'll let him know that more is possible. You'll also give him the encouragement he needs to keep going.

Allow for Changes

I tell my students that we set goals so that we know when to stop. In an achievement-crazed community, that principle is crucial to survival. Sometimes, however, the goals we set turn out to be not as perfectly formed as we had hoped. In those cases, reassessment is necessary and indicates a healthy level of involvement and awareness. Goals change as success changes. After all, we set goals to achieve success, so the very act of goal-setting is an act of defining success. Success is personal and therefore can change.

Some of my students come in believing so little of themselves that they can only hope to survive the test. Their goals reflect that lack of self-confidence: "I will stay calm during the test," "I will finish the whole test." Other students inform me that they will not be happy until they achieve a perfect score. Their goals are often not only unrealistic, but are not based on any sense of what is needed for admission to a top school.

As preparation continues, parents and students can reassess the level of achievement that they hope to reach. Whether the initial goals were too high, too low, too specific, or entirely off base, they can be adjusted to better reflect the reality of the student's testing ability and progress.

Be careful! Too many times, over-obsessed parents have refused to accept victory. I've seen, time and time again, an overworked and overextended child struggle to reach an ever-receding goal, as each time she achieved the aspired-to score, her mother pushed it higher. I've heard too often, "Well, if you were able to raise your score 100 points, you can do it again." I've seen kids earn acceptances to their top choice schools, only to have their parents push them to try for higher ranked, more competitive options. The goal can't be infinity; there has to be an agreed-upon point at which to declare victory.

Communicate

I like to ask parents what their goals are, and then ask the kids separately, to compare answers. Actually, kids are pretty honest. I can ask teens, "What is your goal for this test? And what is your father's?" They'll tell me, and they'll report how much pressure they're receiving to achieve their parents' goals. But, sometimes they'll claim that their parents are pretty laid back, yet I'm fielding three phone calls a week from the kid's micromanaging mother.

It's nice to want your child to do well, but you can't have goals for your child if your child does not share them. They won't happen and resentment will fester. If you're working on one goal and the kid's working on another, there will be constant destructive friction. Worse, often these goals are unstated or unclear, which ensures that they won't be reached.

A lot of kids just give up under that situation, which is a bad result for everyone involved. I've seen many students struggle to convince their parents to let them work in their own way, achieve their own goals, and then give up under the effort. I've seen far too many just stop trying altogether, reasoning that if they can't be successful in the way they want to, they just won't try at all.

Communicate your goals, but more importantly, listen. And listen first. SAT success should not be a power struggle, and parents who push too hard and listen too little rob their children of their best allies. Your children know that their best friends all want higher scores and that the only people who truly are on their side are you, their parents.

When you are discussing goals, start with core values and interests. Find areas in which you and your child agree. We value working hard. We value achievement. We value honesty. We are interested in bioengineering. We are interested in a specific school. We value personal attention and coziness in a university. We are interested in a high-ranking school to make the path to medical school easier. Figure out what is informing your desire for a high score.

Take a minute with or without your child, and write down what your core values and interests are as you navigate the college admissions process. What is it specifically that you hope to gain from the experience? What kinds of values and experiences do you want your child to have in college? What specific factors are most critical to you? Just the process of spelling this out will tell you a lot about what you need to do next.

The thing about values and interests is that there are many paths to success. If you choose your path before you choose your interests, you are stuck in a course that may not lead to personal fulfillment and may not be possible to achieve. It's also a lot easier to negotiate based on interests rather than on positions. For example, your son values an active Greek life, and you value an on-campus ministry. Rather than your son locking in on University of Florida and you on Holy Cross, you can together seek out schools that provide your child both opportunities.

Learning to talk about interests and values instead of positions is tricky. One suggestion: if your child wants University of Florida, say, "That's an interesting choice. Could you help me understand what it is that makes you interested in that school?" If the answer is that there are really hot girls in the campus brochure, you can discount his opinion accordingly. He may, however, surprise you. Maybe it's the first-class entomology program there, or maybe it's the football team.

It could, and often is, a misconception or a deeper issue that leads to a child's staunch position. He may think that the school offers amenities found nowhere else. He may have been told that he's not smart enough to go to Ivy League schools, or he may be afraid to go far from home. Find out his interests, and if some are misconceptions, then work to debunk them. Visit other schools, talk about other factors, and discuss how they might affect his decision. Above all, make it clear that it is his decision within certain guidelines, and that you will

VALUES WORKSHEET

_____

_____

_____

_____

_____

_____

_____

_____

_____

_____

_____

_____

_____

_____

_____

_____

_____

_____

_____

_____

_____

_____

_____

support him throughout his college years (emotionally, that is—you're not obligated to shell out for his frat dues).

OUR GOALS AS PARENTS

As parents, we all want the best for our children. We want our children to be successful. We may even feel that we want to *give* them success. There is, however, a twist: the goal of all parents should be to develop within their children the attributes and skills they need in order to make themselves successful. It is perilously easy to conflate that with just making their kids successful.

In academics, it is too easy to reward the grades rather than the habits that get the grades. (Ever hear of students cheating to get the grade?) Do I help my son write a better paper or do I help him be a better writer? I see far too many students far too focused on numbers, and far too incapable of building their own successes.

Are you helping your child develop good study habits or doing her homework for her? Parents tell me, "But these grades matter!" Which is true, but do they really matter as much as your daughter's confidence in herself? And, if parents start early in essentially giving success to their children, it is immeasurably difficult to imagine a definitive cutoff at which to stop. Once he is into the right high school? The right college? The right job? The right house?

Children have to be allowed to fail in order to learn. The point of falling down is in learning to pick yourself up. Applaud the picking up. Talk about the things that matter for success and teach those to your children. Remember, if we know what leads to success and we teach those skills, or instill those attributes, we will get success. Rather, our children will build their own success. If we focus on the success only, we risk giving short shrift to those inputs. In the long term, we willingly sacrifice a short-term win, even embracing a loss, if we learn from it, improve our fundamentals, and improve our long-term prospects for success.

***

I met with Rory beginning in his sophomore year. As we talked through his grades (A's) and PSAT scores (equivalent of 600 verbal and 640 math on the old SAT), we talked about the schools he had

some interest in. "Stanford" was the first name that jumped from his
lips. "Great school," I replied, "and what Stanford is looking for is
scores in the 700s, preferably over 2200 total." Facts. The basis of
Rory's plan.

A goal without a plan is a wish, as I explained to Rory. Don't count on luck, a rich uncle, the cavalry, or a fairy godmother. We all know (or think we do) of someone who got into the school of our dreams with a less-than-stellar profile, whether it be low grades, low test scores, or a poor essay. The truth is, however, that there is likely some rather private fact that accounts for that student's successful admission—he is a legacy, he is the top lacrosse player in the region, his mother's college roommate is the current university president. Your plan must be based on facts, objective criteria over which you have some control.

So Rory's scores were about 100 points lower than he needed for the school of his dreams. But, he had done the first three steps. He had identified a goal: Stanford. He had put it on paper: he had his tentative college list with Stanford on top. He had gotten the real facts: he knew what he had and what he needed in pure numbers, on paper. Rory was a really bright guy. I had no doubt that he was capable of reaching his goal—this was important, that he and I both believed that he could. If you believe you can do it, then you probably can. If you believe you cannot, then you are also probably right.

So, we started to break down Rory's scores. What were the issues? What was holding him back? As a really academic guy, Rory brought considerable skills to the SAT. However, he also brought deeply in-grained patterns. We started by talking about what the test measures, and more importantly, what it doesn't measure. Rory seemed shocked by how strongly he was affected by the SAT. He began to understand how the structure of the test was misleading him, discouraging him, and ultimately robbing him of points. "What kind of racket is this?" he kept asking.

I articulated my view of the limitations of the test and how, in College Board's quest for the perfectly reliable bell curve, something often has to give. Frequently that something has academically able students getting scores well out of alignment with their school performance. For Rory, that meant he needed to learn everything about the test, its patterns and his patterns, and make sure he lined up those patterns correctly. He needed to start thinking like ETS and being active in his test preparation and performance.

Step two was that as well read as Rory was, there were still many words on the SAT that he didn't know or didn't know well enough for the purpose of the SAT. So, Rory and I set up a course of study so that he came to learn every word, or nearly every word, that had popped up on the SAT in recent years. He studied those words daily, faithfully. Rory was going to be sure that if he didn't get into Stanford, it wouldn't be because of ten esoteric words he didn't know. He learned hundreds and hundreds of words. It was an achievable and measurable goal.

Step three was to make a team, Rory's team. Socrates was reported to be the wisest man in the ancient world. Because he openly professed how little he knew, he persistently put himself in a position to learn from everyone he met. This is hard for teenagers and can be just as hard for parents. In Rory's case, he and his family had sought out the help of a highly regarded educational counselor, who had put him in touch with me. As capable as Rory was, he got his answers much faster with the help of people who already knew the terrain.

Working together on Rory's team, with Rory and his parents, was exciting and exhilarating. I watched Rory come to understand himself and understand the SAT. I watched him learn how to set and achieve goals. I watched him overcome a persistent problem with underperformance, and I watched him celebrate his victory with a well-earned sense of pride. When Rory finally got his Stanford acceptance letter, it was a secondary, and somehow less important, victory.

Afterword

"We are what we repeatedly do. Excellence, then, is not an act but a habit," wrote Aristotle many centuries ago. This aphorism is the motto of our tutoring company and is a great message for kids and for parents. Success is not one great performance, one game-winning touchdown, or one standardized test. Failure is not one poor grade or one low score. Academic success is found in strong grades week after week, year after year. Likewise, good parenting is found in the messages and lessons we give our children every day. We should teach our young people to develop the habits that lead to success: set goals; know yourself; work hard; appreciate feedback. Treat failure, said Henry Ford, as an opportunity to begin anew, but more intelligently.

The SAT is a high-stakes test. For admission to many colleges, it does matter. But this test is not a measure of a child's worth. It's just a test, one of many. It doesn't prove her to be smart or him to be incapable. Neither does it validate or invalidate our abilities as parents. We can help our children to be successful on the SAT while still acting in ways consistent with our values and with what we teach our children is really important. We can all navigate this test while always placing our concern for our children above our concern for our children's success.

At the end of the day, at the end of the test, high score or low, the sun will rise tomorrow. With or without the laurel on their heads, the coveted scores on transcripts, or the admission letter of choice, your children will still have homework to do, practices to attend, and then, like you, jobs to do and dreams to follow. We wish your child every success on the SAT. More importantly, we wish your child every success in following his dreams and fulfilling his potential.

Works Cited

Abrams, Samuel J. "Unflagged SATs." *Education Next* (Summer 2005). http://www.educationnext.org (accessed May 2006).

Batcha, Becky. "Test Anxiety: The Education Controversy That's Gripping the Nation." *Child* (September 2005): 160 (interview with Macario Guajardo).

Blanchard, Ken, and Spencer Johnson. *The One-Minute Manager.* New York: William Morrow, 1981.

Covey, Stephen R. *The Seven Habits of Highly Effective People.* New York: Free Press, 1990.

Gladwell, Malcolm. *Blink.* New York: Little, Brown, 2005.

Gladwell, Malcolm. "The Art of Failure." *New Yorker,* April 21 and 28, 2000. http://www.malcolmgladwell.com (accessed May 2, 2006).

Lemann, Nicholas. *The Big Test: The Secret History of the American Meritocracy.* New York: Farrar, Straus & Giroux, 1999.

Perlstein, Linda. "Grammar Glitch Pushes PSAT to Rethink, Rescore." *Washington Post,* May 14, 2003, p. A01.

Steele, C. M., and J. Aronson. "Stereotype Threat and the Intellectual Test Performance of African-Americans." *Journal of Personality and Social Psychology* 69 (1995): 797–811.

Wahlstrom, Kyla. "Changing Times: Findings from the First Longitudinal Study of Later High School Start Times." *NASSP Bulletin* 86, no. 633 (December 2002).

Winerip, Michael. "SAT Essay Test Rewards Length and Ignores Errors of Fact." *New York Times,* May 4, 2005.

Wolfson, Amy R. and Mary A. Carskadon. "Sleep Schedules and Daytime Functioning in Adolescents." *Child Development* 69, no. 4 (1998): 875–87.

Notes

CHAPTER 1

1. If you combine all the haystacks, you'll have one really big haystack. There are twelve stamps in a dozen, no matter the cent value per stamp. There is no dirt in a hole. If all but two died, then only those two are left. One coin is not a nickel, it's a quarter; the other coin is a nickel.
2. See http://senatorlavalle.com/press_archive_story.asp?id=13615 (accessed Sept. 2006).
3. Karen W. Arenson, "Class-Action Lawsuit to Be Filed over SAT Scoring Errors," *New York Times*, April 9, 2006, late ed., sec. 1, p. 33.
4. See http://www.cnn.com/2006/EDUCATION/08/29/sat.scores.ap/index. html (accessed Sept. 2006).
5. Nicholas Lemann, *The Big Test: The Secret History of the American Meritocracy* (New York: Farrar, Straus & Giroux, 1999).
6. The SAT was officially born around 1926, an offspring of the Army Intelligence Tests administered during World War I. ETS didn't arrive on the scene until 1947, however; see Lemann, *The Big Test*, pp. 30–1.

CHAPTER 2

1. For a more complete discussion of this claim, look for the section entitled "Development of Achievement Motivation," coauthored by Allan Wigfield, Jacquelynne S. Eccles, Ulrich Schiefele, Robert Roeser, and Pamela Davis-Kean in W. Damon and N. Eisenberg, vol. ed., *Handbook of Child Psychology, 6th ed. vol. 3, Social, Emotional, and Personality Development* (New York: John Wiley, 2006).
2. For more information, see http://www.singlesexschools.org/research-learning.htm.

CHAPTER 4

1. As of summer 2006, a large percentage of universities still had not decided exactly what to do with the essay score or, indeed, the entire writing score of the new SAT. Many explain that they are waiting for a few years of statistical analysis in order to ensure that the writing score has predictive ability—in other words, no one is quite sure yet that a great writing score means that a student will actually do well in college.

2. If all of these tests sound foreign to you, don't worry. The SAT has emerged in different forms throughout the years, but you and your child need only worry about today's tests. Talk to your child's guidance counselor about other admissions tests that colleges might require, such as the SAT IIs (the old Achievement Tests) and the ACT.

3. In an article in the *Washington Post* (May 14, 2003, p. A01) entitled "Grammar Glitch Pushes PSAT to Rethink, Rescore," Linda Perlstein discussed how an English teacher spotted a grammatical error on a PSAT question ETS had scored as error-free. ETS, upon consideration, conceded that the question did, in fact, contain an error.

4. Michael Winerip, "SAT Essay Test Rewards Length and Ignores Errors of Fact," *New York Times*, May 4, 2005.

CHAPTER 5

1. Within three days of an SAT administration, a student can cancel his or her scores by contacting ETS and requesting that particular test not be scored.

2. Richard Bach, *Illusions: The Adventures of a Reluctant Messiah* (New York: Dell Publishing, 1977).

3. At most elite universities, freshman class size has remained stable for the past ten or so years while the number of applicants has doubled, tripled, or quadrupled. Each year schools report a new record number of applicants, and for a few of the top-tier schools, admissions rates have dropped below ten percent.

4. Becky Batcha, "Test Anxiety: The Education Controversy that's Gripping the Nation," *Child* (September 2005): 160 (interview with Macario Guajardo).

5. For more about "stereotype threat," see Claude Steele's research. C. M. Steele and J. Aronson, "Stereotype Threat and the Intellectual Test Performance of African-Americans," *Journal of Personality and Social Psychology* 69 (1995): 797–811.

6. For a great discussion on choking versus panicking, see Malcolm Gladwell, "The Art of Failure," *New Yorker*, April 21 and 28, 2000, http://www.malcolmgladwell.com (accessed May 2006).
7. Definition taken from www.merriam-webster.com.
8. David Miller, "Sleep Deprivation and Learning," http://www.apa.org/ed/topss/dmiller.html (accessed May 2006).
9. Amy R. Wolfson and Mary A. Carskadon, "Sleep Schedules and Daytime Functioning in Adolescents," *Child Development* 69, no. 4 (1998): 875–87.
10. For a summary of the study, see Kyla Wahlstrom, "Changing Times: Findings from the First Longitudinal Study of Later High School Start Times," *NASSP Bulletin* 86, no. 633 (December 2002).

CHAPTER 7

1. The ETS website is www.ets.org.
2. Jane Gross, "Paying for a Disability Diagnosis to Gain Time on College Boards" (November 2002), www.aapd-dc.org/News/disability/gaintime-onSAT.html (accessed July 2006).
3. For a more thorough discussion, see "Does Loophole Give Rich Kids More Time on SAT?" by Jake Tapper, Dan Morris, and Lara Setrakian, at ABC News *Nightline* website, http://abcnews.go.com/Nightline/story?id=1787712&page=1 (accessed August 2006).
4. For more information, see Samuel J. Abrams' fascinating article "Unflagged SATs," comparing score data for standard and special circumstance examinees before and after ETS unflagged the SAT scores. This 2005 article is available on the Hoover Institute's website, http://www.educationnext.org (accessed May 2006).

CHAPTER 8

1. Stephen R. Covey, *The Seven Habits of Highly Effective People* (New York: Free Press, 1990).

CHAPTER 9

1. Malcolm Gladwell, *Blink* (New York: Little, Brown, 2005).

CHAPTER 10

1. Ken Blanchard and Spencer Johnson, *The One-Minute Manager* (New York: William Morrow and Company, 1981).

CHAPTER 12

1. For further elucidation of some of these ideas about goal setting, see Brian Tracy's work at www.briantracy.com.

Index